The Fire Is Back!

It must not be forgotten where the ultimate power to change is and always has been — in the head, hands and hearts of the educators who work in our schools.

(Sirotnik, 1989, p. 113)

The school as the center of change. In Thomas Sergiovanni and John H. Moore (Eds.) (1989). *Schooling for tomorrow: Directing reforms to issues that count* (pp. 89-113). Boston: Allyn & Bacon.

**CORWIN
PRESS**

The Corwin Press logo—a raven striding across an open book—
represents the happy union of courage and learning. We are a
professional-level publisher of books and journals for K-12 educators, and we are committed to creating and providing resources
that embody these qualities. Corwin's motto is "Success for All
Learners."

The Fire Is Back!

Principals Sharing School Governance

Jo Blase
Joseph Blase

CORWIN PRESS, INC.
A Sage Publications Company
Thousand Oaks, California

For information address:

SAGE Publications, Inc.
2455 Teller Road
Thousand Oaks, California 91320
E-mail: order@corwin.sagepub.com

CORWIN
PRESS

SAGE Publications Ltd.
6 Bonhill Street
London EC2A 4PU
United Kingdom

SAGE Publications India Pvt. Ltd.
M-32 Market
Greater Kailash I
New Delhi 110 048 India

Printed in the United States of America

Library of Congress Cataloging-in-Publication Data

Main entry under title:
Blase, Jo Roberts.
   The fire is back: principals sharing school governance / authors,
Jo Blase, Joseph Blase.
      p. cm.
   Includes bibliographical references and index.
   ISBN 0-8039-6332-7 (pbk.: acid-free paper). — ISBN 0-8039-6331-9
(cloth: acid-free paper)
   1. Teacher participation in administration—United States.
2. Student participation in administration—United States.
3. Community and school—United States. 4. School principals—
United States. 5. School management and organization—United
States. I. Blase, Joseph. II. Title.
LB2806.45.B52 1996
371.2′00973—dc20   96-25181

97 98 99 00 01 02 03 10 9 8 7 6 5 4 3 2 1

Acquiring Editor: Gracia Alkema
Editorial Assistant: Kristen Green
Production Editor: Sherrise Purdum
Typesetter / Designer: Marion S. Warren

Contents

Foreword

This volume serves both scholars and practitioners well, as the voices of exemplary shared governance principals are heard. *The Fire Is Back! Principals Sharing School Governance* vividly portrays exemplary principals' perspectives on shared governance leadership in several schools that belong to the League of Professional Schools. Professors Blase and Blase bring fresh insights to these perspectives, placing them in the context of the educational reform movement and current thinking about schools as organizations. They outline both the role of the principal in newly restructured schools and the effect of shared governance on the organization. The authors point out that this new shared governance model requires principals to accept criticism, deal with ambiguity, and trust and treat teachers as professionals by creating a supportive work environment in which they can take chances and risk failure. Shared governance principals recognize that it is the strong leader who encourages teachers to be autonomous and take creative risks. As one of the interviewed principals explained, "One leads by developing the talent and commitment of others rather than gaining their compliance to rules."

The effective schools literature demonstrated that in schools identified as particularly successful, principals involved teachers, parents, and, occasionally, secondary school students in day-to-day decision making. However, the research provided insufficient insight into how principals in these schools went about sharing decision making and enhancing involvement. As a result, it was unclear how these schools became successful. Furthermore, reform debates of the past decade have had a tendency to stay on the rhetorical level; they, too, have offered little specific guidance for practitioners. Debates have focused, for example, on whether participation and shared governance are likely to be "fads" that come and go in schools.

Blase and Blase provide a much needed link in the literature. In this book, one finds little in the way of speculation concerning whether participation is simply a transitory phenomenon. Indeed, the authors offer specific guidance about promising practices that would seemingly guarantee participatory decision making as a more permanent occurrence in schools. The book integrates discussions about theoretical concepts (e.g., instruction and leadership) with the perspectives of practicing principals who have been successful in shared governance experiments. These perspectives are candid and personal, which the reader will enjoy. The book also examines what the perspectives of exemplary principals illustrate about fundamental notions of power, authority, and participation in school organizations.

From their unique vantage point, Blase and Blase's contribution to the literature is a realistic portrayal of the complexity and fragility of shared governance arrangements. The authors denote that sharing power is not something that principals can do rashly or recklessly; instead, it must be carried out carefully and wisely. Blase and Blase detail the extraordinary effort and thinking that goes into making a shared governance effort exemplary. Shared governance principals are reflective practitioners who constantly revisit (and are not averse to second-guessing) their decisions. They continuously assess whether they should change their management strategies, for example, to be more consistent with their own definitions of shared governance and participation. However, it is clear from the book that to view principals as simply turning over the school to others belies the complexity of the process. Just as a teacher who wants to encourage student participation does not simply turn over the classroom to students, these principals are careful and strategic about how they introduce participation and specify which areas of decision making participation receive priority.

What knowledge do we gain about power and authority from the book? Blase and Blase observe that, through shared governance, principals realized that "shared power was power enhanced." As one principal said, "Because I'm not controlling everything, the school is actually in better control than it ever was. We talk about *all being in the same soup*, being in this together. There's more power to share, not less, and the pie has grown bigger." As Tannenbaum observed some time ago, "through participation, management increases its control by giving up some of its authority" (cited in Pugh and Hickson, 1983, *Great Writers on Organizations*). Blase and Blase convincingly maintain that the shared governance model does not eliminate the principal's position; in fact, it enhances it. Instead of controlling others, principals focus, among other things, on supporting the school's mission, encouraging interdependence among teachers, and fostering school-community relationships.

Readers will come away from this book with a clear sense of "what happens" when a principal decides to adopt a participatory, shared governance model of school management. Through principals' accounts, readers can understand "what happens" to the school organization as well as to the principals themselves and their own sense of career development. They acquire insight into both the personal satisfaction realized, and the dilemmas and paradoxes confronted, in successful restructuring. Finding ways of resolving dilemmas and paradoxes, the authors maintain, becomes the basis for principals' personal growth. The observations of three principals illustrate both tensions and accomplishments as follows: One said, "I am conscious of when I make a decision that I shouldn't have made myself . . . when I have violated shared governance principles. I have grown professionally." Another commented, "Now teachers are not afraid to come to me and say, 'This is what I think we should do.' And our conflict is good conflict." Finally, one said, in words inspiring the book's title, "[Shared governance] helps me get up and come to work every day—I'm excited! . . . I've always loved schools. . . . For a few years, though, I really struggled, but now *the fire is back!*"

Sharon Conley
University of California
Santa Barbara

Reference

Pugh, D. S., & Hickson, D. J. (1993). *Great writers on organizations*. Brookfield, VT: Dartmouth.

Preface

*The overriding ethical considerations that principals must address
involve how to fulfill their responsibility for moving schools forward
without imposing their way upon teachers and how to honor teacher
beliefs while remaining true to their beliefs.*
                                                    —Reitzug (1994, p. 305)

This book is written for practicing and prospective principals who
want to restructure schools through shared decision making. It
is based on a study of how exemplary principals practice facilita-
tive/democratic leadership and what their thoughts and feelings are
in confronting the challenges of such leadership.

Attempts to restructure American schools—to initiate and implement school-based collaborative processes as a means of achieving greater effectiveness and productivity—have increased greatly
in the past several years. Unfortunately, many of these attempts
have faltered because of a lack of research-based knowledge to guide
such efforts. *The Fire Is Back! Principals Sharing School Governance*
helps fill this crucial knowledge gap. This book is the third in our
trilogy of books based on several studies of facilitative/democratic
principal leadership. As such, it provides a valuable companion to
Empowering Teachers: What Successful Principals Do (Blase &

Blase, 1994), which describes teachers' perspectives on empowering principals' leadership, and *Democratic Principals in Action: Eight Pioneers* (Blase, Blase, Anderson, & Dungan, 1995), which presents case studies of shared-governance principals in a variety of school contexts.

The study discussed in this book offers new empirically grounded knowledge, both descriptive and conceptual, about shared governance from the perspectives of exemplary shared-governance principals. Presented in a systematic, thematic format that includes relevant current research, this book offers the first research-based account of the actual experiences of exemplary principals in shared-governance schools.

The Fire Is Back! Principals Sharing School Governance focuses on exemplary principals of schools affiliated with the League of Professional Schools (Glickman, 1993). The book discusses the principals' views on shared governance and democratic schooling; the excitement and challenges of becoming involved in collaborative decision making among teachers, parents, and students; and the principals' feelings and professional growth as they strive to become "one among equals" with their colleagues.

What does facilitative/democratic leadership look like? What do principals who practice such leadership actually do, think, and feel when collaborative decision making becomes a school goal? This book provides new knowledge about these and related questions. Chapter 1 presents a brief overview of the professional literature on facilitative/democratic leadership. It also describes the personal definitions of shared governance as discussed by the principals we studied. Chapter 2 discusses the impetus for and initiation of shared-governance efforts in various school contexts. Chapter 3 discusses how principals achieve "virtuosity" in leadership through a new set of beliefs, the use of five primary strategies, and profound reflection.

In Chapters 4 and 5 we examine the practical considerations of fundamental structural changes that drive shared-governance initiatives. We also discuss effective strategies that the principals we studied used for involving parents and students in school-based decision making. How exemplary shared-governance principals promote a common vision and maintain a focus on instructional matters are key leadership strategies discussed in Chapters 6 and 7. In Chapter 8, we chronicle the principals' thoughts and feelings—including challenging, rewarding, and even spiritual events.

The importance of principals' openness to feedback and ability to learn from experience is discussed in Chapter 9. Chapter 10, the final chapter, summarizes the findings and conclusions of our study and explores its implications for prospective and practicing principals (and teachers) in terms of *readiness* to enact the role of a facilitative/democratic leader. This chapter also highlights principals' personal advice about shared governance. Research methods and procedures are described in Resource A. Throughout this book, we have used italics freely to emphasize important points, both in our writing and in quotations from the principals we studied. When italics appear in quotations from other researchers, we indicate whether the emphasis is ours or that of the other author(s).

In many ways, the principals studied in this book are the opposite of traditional/authoritarian principals. Virtues such as sharing, openness, trust, and respect for others—virtues we found to be the essence of facilitative/democratic leadership—are often the antithesis of traditional/authoritarian leadership. The principals we describe lack the dominant presence of traditional principals precisely because they have rejected a preoccupation with self, the imposition of their personal vision on others, and the traditional authoritarian quest for power. These principals have the courage and skill to work with others as equals, to be one among equals, and to place the vision and power of the group far above their personal needs and goals. They do not seek the limelight; their lives are characterized by dignity, honesty, and courage.

Indeed, the research we have done during the past several years indicates that a new democratic ideal of the principal-leader is emerging. It is an ideal founded in the notion of empowering others to increase their capacity and commitment to do their best for education. This book is about such principals, special people who believe in democratic participation among teachers, parents, and students. It is about the crucial role that exemplary principals play in enabling a school to become a model of democracy. In "Democracy, Public Schools, and the Politics of Education," Dayton (1995) explains:

> In view of public schools' vital role in inculcating democratic values, and of the utilitarian, humanitarian, and egalitarian benefits of a democratic education, what constitutes good education in a democratic nation should be in significant part determined

by a pragmatic assessment of whether this education enables public schools to effectively teach and practice democratic principles. (p. 137)

Clearly, the shared-governance principals we studied have decided *they can do no less.*

References

Blase, J., & Blase, J. R. (1994). *Empowering teachers: What successful principals do.* Thousand Oaks, CA: Corwin.

Blase, J., Blase, J., Anderson, G., & Dungan, S. (1995). *Democratic principals in action: Eight pioneers.* Thousand Oaks, CA: Corwin.

Dayton, J. (1995). Democracy, public schools, and the politics of education. *Review Journal of Philosophy and Social Science, XX*(1), 135-156.

Glickman, C. (1993). *Renewing America's schools: A guide for school-based action.* San Francisco: Jossey-Bass.

Reitzug, U. C. (1994). A case study of empowering principal behavior. *American Educational Research Journal, 31*(2), 283-307.

Acknowledgments

We are deeply indebted not only to the shared-governance principals who participated in the study that formed the basis of this book—and who must remain nameless—but also to the practitioners and professors who generously contributed their valuable time to reviews of early drafts of this book: Julie Graham, Faye Jones, Margaret Jones, Kathy Kelley, Mary O'Hair, and Janna Penn. As in all of our research projects on shared governance, Lew Allen provided thoughtful commentary and assistance. We also appreciate the superb technical support of our secretaries, Donna Bell and Linda Edwards; our editor, Cheryl Smith; and our research assistants, Steve Black, Doug Dixon, and Susan Walker.

About the Authors

Jo Blase is an Associate Professor of Educational Leadership at the University of Georgia and a former public school teacher, principal, and director of staff development. She received a PhD in educational administration, curriculum, and supervision in 1983 from the University of Colorado at Boulder. Through work with the Beginning Principal Study National Research Team, the Georgia League of Professional Schools, and educators with whom she consults, she has pursued her interest in how principals prepare for and enter educational and instructional leadership, with an emphasis on supervisory discourse.

Winner of the 1983 American Association of School Administrators Outstanding Research Award, Blase has been published in several journals, including the *Journal of Staff Development,* the *Journal of Curriculum and Supervision,* and the *Alberta Journal of Educational Research.* She has published *Empowering Teachers: What Successful Principals Do* (with Joseph Blase, 1994, Corwin Press) and *Democratic Principals in Action: Eight Pioneers* (with Joseph Blase, Gary Anderson, and Sherry Dungan, 1995, Corwin Press). She has also written chapters on becoming a principal, school renewal, supervision, and organizational development. She is currently conducting research on supervisory discourse among physicians as medical educators.

Joseph Blase is a professor of educational leadership at the University of Georgia. Since he received his PhD in 1980 from Syracuse University, his research has focused entirely on understanding the work lives of teachers. He has published many studies in the areas of teacher stress, relations between teachers' personal and professional lives, teacher socialization, and principal-teacher relationships. His recent work is focused on school-level micropolitics; earlier work in the same area received the 1988 Davis Memorial Award given by the University Council for Educational Administration.

Blase edited *The Politics of Life in Schools: Power, Conflict, and Cooperation* (Sager, 1991; winner of the 1994 Critic's Choice Award sponsored by the American Education Studies Association, 1991, Sage); coauthored, with Peggy Kirby, *Bringing Out the Best in Teachers: What Effective Principals Do* (1992, Corwin Press); coauthored, with Jo Blase, *Empowering Teachers: What Successful Principals Do* (1994, Corwin Press); coauthored, with Jo Blase, Gary Anderson, and Sherry Dungan, *Democratic Principals in Action: Eight Pioneers* (1995, Corwin Press); and coauthored, with Gary Anderson, *The Micropolitics of Educational Leadership* (1995).

To Schnook and to Mom and Dad

1

The Meaning of Shared Governance in a Variety of School Contexts

A democratic theory of education recognizes the importance of empowering citizens to make educational policy and also of constraining their choices among policies in accordance with those principles of nonrepression and nondiscrimination that preserve the intellectual and social foundations of democratic deliberations. A society that empowers citizens to make educational policy, moderated by these two principled constraints, realizes the democratic ideal of education.

—Gutman (1987, p. 14)

Principals in recently restructured schools have new and varied roles. Much of their work involves developing professional relationships with new types of teachers who are empowered to carry out many of the tasks previously relegated to the principals. In restructured schools, principals who were once responsible for program administration are now charged with facilitating, enabling, motivating, and coordinating the empowered professionals in their buildings. In addition, principals in restructured schools are changing their relationships with external communities and constituencies. They are becoming flag bearers, enterprising external leaders, as well as boundary spanners as they coordinate the total school environment.

—Rallis & Goldring (1994, p. 1)

Today's educational leader operates in a climate of school restructuring and reform wherein bureaucratic structures are fast giving way to collaborative endeavors among groups of education professionals. We are finding, from a spate of reform efforts and studies of those efforts, that school reform is a complex and ambiguous process. It requires that a principal let go of old roles and power while being accountable for decisions made by others.

Redefining one's leadership role can be challenging and stressful. In this case it necessitates the development of collaborative decision-making processes, the creation of a shared vision, and the invention of a supportive network of professional relationships. This book seeks to expand knowledge of the experiences of exemplary shared-governance principals as they each strive to become "one among equals," a leader among leaders, and to create a community of learners. We have found that in that striving, these principals discover that *the fire is back!*

The Empowering Principal's Behaviors: Shared Governance of Schools

Principals who embrace teacher professionalism do more than share power: They *multiply* it. This is akin to the concept of "leadership density" (Sergiovanni, 1987), which describes principals who free, encourage, and energize others to join the leadership process. Principals who are empowering are far from being mild "psychobabblers"; King and Kerchner (1991, pp. 6-9) found that they are "pragmatists with vision":

1. They are entrepreneurial, gathering and *redistributing resources* and encouraging others to do so.
2. They realize that one leads best by *developing the talent and commitment* of others rather than gaining their compliance through rules; indeed, old bureaucracies consider them "dangerously independent."
3. They *view themselves as empowered* because of better communication and shared responsibilities.
4. They *admit that they do not have all the answers.*

5. They are comfortable enough to allow the staff to "win" on issues; they encourage full discussions, fair decisions, and effective implementation even when they disagree.
6. They *provide symbolic leadership* (e.g., gestures of support, awards, statements of principles and values, slogans and stories) to develop a culture of collaboration.
7. They are *statespersons,* providing an example of principled, moral leadership.
8. They rely on personal *leadership rather than positional authority* by working collaboratively and delegating authority.

Neufeld and Freeman (1992) found that the following principal behaviors significantly enhance teachers' sense of empowerment:

♦ Trusting and treating teachers as professionals
♦ Creating a nonrestrictive work environment in which teachers can take chances and risk failures
♦ Exhibiting a leadership style that is neither dogmatic nor autocratic
♦ Inviting divergent points of view
♦ Giving teachers a clear voice in decision making

In essence, education researchers contend that the principal's actions—*his or her readiness to share power; ability to provide appropriate processes, information, and resources*; and *leadership skills*—determine the extent, nature, and pattern of participation, or shared governance, in their schools (Chapman, 1988; Duke, Showers, & Imber, 1980).

Defining Empowerment

Several educational theorists focusing on shared governance (i.e., teacher empowerment, shared decision making, site-based decision making) have produced concise definitions of empowerment that have numerous dimensions. For example, according to Short and Rinehart (1992), empowerment is a *process* including participative decision making, teacher impact, professional autonomy, professional development opportunities, and a sense of self-efficacy; empowerment enables participants to assume responsibility for their own growth and for decisions about their work and practice.

Bredeson (1994) defines empowerment as autonomy that others perceive to be a *process,* a *sense* of identity, and an *opportunity* for autonomous professional behavior, and as a professional work *environment.* Similarly, Lightfoot (1986) defines empowerment as "the opportunities a person has for autonomy, responsibility, choice, and authority" (p. 9). She makes the following *assumptions* about empowerment (pp. 9-10):

1. Opportunities for empowerment must begin early, be carefully designed to match the intellectual, psychic, and moral maturity of the person, and be *acted on.*
2. The expression of empowerment in schools should be felt at every level—by *students, teachers,* and *administrators* [we would add *parents*].
3. Empowerment reflects a *dynamic process,* not a static final state. . . . One expects an *ethos* of self-criticism, dialogue, and even discomfort as the members of the community try to negotiate relationships that will allow initiative, autonomy, and responsibility for all. One expects a riveting *tension* between individual will and choice, on the one hand, and the requirements of community cohesion and commitment, on the other.

Bredeson (1989) was among the early researchers who studied the effects of facilitative principal leadership on teacher empowerment in several restructured schools. He learned that such schools had characteristics associated with effective traditional schools; they had, for example, a positive climate, commitment, professionalism, ownership, and independent problem solving. Bredeson also found several differences from traditional schools, however: a relaxation of hierarchical lines of authority (e.g., teachers speculated that a visitor to the school would not be able to discern who was the principal), a reduction of teacher isolation through high levels of peer interaction and communication, and an openness to working in groups to hear all voices and reach consensus (even though this occasionally produced "more griping and bitching"). In a later study, Bredeson (1995, p. 9) described a school district in which empowerment meant

> an invitation to principals and teachers to empower one another through collaborative work, shared decision making, and shared responsibility on issues of importance.

The norms of empowerment described by Bredeson (1995, p. 8) were supported by nine critical factors:

1. Empowerment was locally defined and was expressed in language and images that made it more concrete than abstract.
2. Levels of comfort with and readiness for empowerment matched school circumstances and individual capacity.
3. The modeling of behaviors consistent with professional empowerment norms started at the top, with the superintendent and other administrators.
4. Time and money were critical resources supporting empowerment.
5. Principals' and teachers' professional roles were greatly expanded both in and beyond the school.
6. Empowerment enhanced teachers' professional image and efficacy.
7. Empowerment tapped the oftentimes underused creative energies and expertise of teachers.
8. Trust and collegiality were norms that created and supported empowerment.
9. Shared power was power enhanced, not power lost.

In the study on which this book is based, we began by asking successful shared-governance principals to discuss what *shared governance* meant to them. Not surprisingly, each principal described shared governance in terms of teacher participation and empowerment (see Figure 1.1).

Perhaps the most critical aspect of empowerment is teacher voice. Indeed, Lightfoot (1986) contends that the effective schools literature defines school effectiveness far too *narrowly*—as "instructional effectiveness"—and thus "neglect[s] the voices, perspectives, and wisdom of school people" who need "power to speak . . . and reveal the dynamics of their achievements" (p. 13).

From his doctoral dissertation research at the University of Georgia, Allen (1993) learned that teachers saw their school's implementation of shared governance as a way to have a voice in instructional and curricular decision making.

Indeed, Kreisberg (1992), a prominent empowerment theorist, placed teacher voice at the very *heart* of teacher empowerment; he stressed breaking the isolation that surrounds teachers' professional experiences. Nias (1989) has shown that teachers who have been given opportunities to enter into dialogues with other teachers and administrators, to assume leadership roles, and to take an active role in developing policies and setting goals (thus giving voice to their concerns, ideas, and reflections) realize greater influence outside the classroom.

As teachers gain voice, their participation levels in decision-making processes tend to change. Crockenberg and Clark (1979) identified five levels of teacher involvement in decision making:

1. Recommendation: Teachers advise the principal.
2. Information: Representative teachers relay the principal's decisions.
3. Consultation: The principal consults with teachers before making decisions.
4. Approval: Representatives alter, approve, or reject the principal's decisions.
5. Authorization: Teacher representatives make decisions.

Crockenberg and Clark also found that involvement in decisions varied according to the nature of an issue, the degree to which the teachers' interests were affected, and the teachers' willingness to take risks connected with assuming responsibility for decisions.

Interestingly, Allen (1993, p. 171) also found that even when teacher participation in school decision making is encouraged, some teachers do not readily accept invitations to voice their thoughts. He

text continues on page 9

Elementary School Principals

Principal A: To me, shared governance is the act of allowing others to share in the decision-making process of any organization. Before, we knew where we wanted to go, as administrators; we kind of led the teachers in our direction: Now, as leaders we have to be honest and say to ourselves, "If we really, truly want teachers to make decisions, if we want them to feel professional, then we've got to go with their judgments." You've got to give up the power. . . . We finally did, but it was not easy. Shared governance is a learning process; the leader must learn to share the decision-making role.

Principal B: Shared governance, to me, means having the decision-making power shared among everybody who is in the school, not just people who are the legal authorities or the appointed administrators. It really means that the governance of a particular institution or body is shared by all of the people who are a part of that body. That includes the teachers, the staff members like the cafeteria workers and the custodians, the parents, all of the stakeholders, including businesspeople from the community. Ideally, it would be shared with the children, too. The decisions we make about the life of the school include curriculum, policy, procedure, budget, textbooks, structure of the day, even parking spaces. Nobody is forced to be involved, but there is an opportunity for everyone who wants to be involved to participate.

Principal C: I am the leader of the school, but the school belongs to all, and all should be involved in the decision-making process. You give it up, you allow others to come in, you listen and let teachers know you are listening. You say, "I believe in you, I trust you."

Middle School Principals

Principal A: Shared governance is where you allow the entire staff to have input into the operation of your school. As a principal, I will never know about everything that needs to be done, so what I try to do is to involve those people who are out there "where the rubber meets the road." *They're out there making the decisions that impact on the kids. Shared governance means equality.*

continued

Figure 1.1. What Shared Governance Means: Principals' Perspectives

Principal B: I think shared governance means making better decisions about instruction because more people who are very closely in tune with instruction are involved in sharing the decision making of the school. For instance, teachers in the classrooms are actually the closest persons to "where the rubber meets the road" in terms of instruction; it's important that they be involved in making decisions because it's their students who will benefit from good decision making.

Principal C: When I became principal of this school, I set a goal of allowing the teachers—*allow* is not a good term—*giving* the teachers an opportunity to affect their workplace. To us, shared governance is teacher involvement in every aspect of the school, particularly within the area of curriculum development and instruction. It's also about the development of the organizational structure for decision making, about the delivery of instruction, and the enhancement of instruction. Instructionally and as educators, we are on the same level. Teachers don't want to be on the same plane as the administrators concerning managerial matters such as working with the superintendent, but they do want to be involved in instructional matters routinely. I foresee a day when teachers observe one another to help each other improve and they collaborate routinely, more than in our present peer-coaching program (which some avail themselves of and some don't).

Principal D: Shared governance is a practical way to solve problems; it works because everybody has an investment in it. There's no risk in initiating ideas anymore, and people don't get sick worrying about what happens if something doesn't work. . . . We do action research every month, and I get more time to be an academic leader because I'm not busy managing custodial or administrative stuff. I even know the kids well; I had time to take a hodgepodge of kids on a bicycle trip to a farm to do some fishing. It was a hoot.

High School Principals

Principal A: Shared governance is a move away from a bureaucratic or an autocratic approach to the governance of schools. When I thought of shared governance initially, I thought in terms of shifting the power for decision making from what was almost exclusively administrators to include other certificated personnel. Now my concept has expanded to include students, other staff members, and parents.

continued

Figure 1.1. Continued

Still, we are struggling with the notion of how much we empower other people. We have a pretty firm grip on how we define involvement of the professional staff, but we start getting a little shaky about others after that. You know, we want to move beyond the old traditional advisory role to actually empowering these other people to be real participants. This is more than just having the ability to exercise power.

Principal B: For 5 years, shared governance for us has included altering our structure slightly from time to time as we have discovered better ways or different ways of doing things. Our structure allows empowered people to have equal voices through equal voting opportunities. The area of decision making in which people in this school have been empowered is schoolwide instructional issues. Teachers do not vote on mops or brooms, nor do they want to. They do not select coaches; that is done by administrators, although we may get some advice from faculty and staff members. I personally also want to involve faculty members in personnel decisions. They have enjoyed being in an advisory capacity on personnel, but they have shied away from the actual decision making about personnel so far.

Figure 1.1. Continued

found that teachers' lack of interest in joining the dialogue was related to six factors (all of which, he noted, could be overcome):

1. The teacher's *background* (personal, professional, or both) discourages the open pressing of a point of view.
2. The *issues* considered are not of interest.
3. The *invitation* is not interpreted as being sincere.
4. *Information* available about the issue is insufficient.
5. The *audience* is intimidating.
6. The specific *setting* and/or the general *structure of the workday* is not considered conducive to expressing one's thoughts.

Does It Work? Early Findings

In their research about the effects of schoolwide action research within the League of Professional Schools, Calhoun and Allen (1994) stated,

> We know that student effects are a difficult bottom line in school improvement. We know that *cultural change* is difficult for our schools. We know that *time* is a long-standing problem, that *overload* of initiatives is a problem, that conscientious use of external *information* by the school as community is rare, that the lack of adequate *staff development* to support organizational goals is common, that the *participation* of students as members of the critical study process is complex, and that the *use of data* to inform practice [constitutes] a major cultural change. Yet with all the known complexities and difficulties, courageous and determined school faculties and districts do make these changes. Each year, the work of League school faculties has been studied; this research has revealed collective movement forward in one or more of these areas [italics added]. (pp. 23-24)

The relationship between teaching conditions and student achievement has, until recently, been somewhat difficult to establish (Murphy & Beck, in press). Elmore (1993) found little empirical evidence that site-based management has any predictable relationship to changes in teaching and learning. However, Hawley (1988) has argued that empowerment (the most common theme of restructuring) *is* linked to *student achievement*. Empowered teachers were better able to do what they know how to do, and support from peers and administrators enabled them to improve their competence.

Recently, Bacharach, Bamberger, Conley, and Bauer (1990) found a positive relationship between teacher decision-making authority and teacher *commitment to school goals* (as well as between teacher decision-making authority and *teacher morale* and teacher *job satisfaction*). The League of Professional Schools' study (Calhoun & Allen, 1994) found that shared-governance initiatives had positive effects on student *academic achievement* and *student behavior,* on *student experiences* in the learning environment, and on *students as participants.* Similarly, a recent study reported by Newmann (1995) linked improvements in student achievement to school restructuring.

It May Be About Leadership

Research also confirms that principals have a positive effect on student performance. Using a path model to determine *which leadership practices make a difference,* Silins (1994) provided empirical evidence for promoting certain leadership behaviors for *school improvement*. These behaviors were operationally defined as being a visionary, providing individual consideration, engaging in collaborative problem solving, ensuring goal achievement, and establishing ethos.

In addition, the work of several researchers suggests that *principal authenticity* with regard to access to knowledge (i.e., enabling teachers by providing them with information, which also demonstrates commitment to teacher leadership) creates a climate more conducive to teacher empowerment, indirectly *influencing student achievement* by promoting a more positive school climate (Bredeson, 1989; Halpin & Croft, 1963; Heck, Larsen, & Marcoulides, 1990; Kirby & Colbert, 1992).

Walking the Talk

Only scant empirical evidence supports the notion that shared decision making has improved student outcomes in shared-governance schools across the United States. In part, this is related to the fact that *shared decision-making models in practice have often not matched the theoretical models*. In other words, they have not been properly implemented. For example, teachers invest time and energy in trivial decisions, are not involved in matters they deem important, act only in an advisory capacity rather than having any real authority in decision making, and are not using or expanding their knowledge base (see Weiss, 1990, for further discussion on this point). We expect significantly improved outcomes for students in schools with properly conceptualized and implemented shared-governance approaches.

Onward!

Inevitably, the results of employing shared decision-making approaches will vary from school to school and will often not meet advocates' expectations or predictions for improved school performance (Smith, 1995). However, the failure of some schools to produce the positive effects of shared decision making on student learning must not deter us from efforts to study, implement, and refine shared-governance initiatives. Beyond all else, we know that

empowered teachers are positive, energetic, and have enthusiasm
for school and for kids. They have ownership in decisions and
support these decisions and their implementation, and they are
prepared to deal with criticism of their decisions. Empowered
teachers are more willing to take on projects, to work together on
teams, to develop consensus building and group process skills.
These teachers are innovative and creative and provide motivation
and support for one another. (Bredeson, 1989, p. 14)

A Tall Order

Currently, the *foundations* of empowerment consist of several
essential elements, including the following:

- *Readiness* to assume more autonomy, responsibility, and
  volunteer work
- *Incrementalism* (trust and morale are built up gradually)
- *Legitimacy* and *ownership* (time and expertise is dedicated
  to substantive, not trivial, issues)
- *Time* and *money* (Bredeson, 1994)

Furthermore, substantive school reform requires that educators
and constituents "move away from a piecemeal approach" (Midgley
& Wood, 1993). This means that the following conditions must apply:

1. Decisions must be linked by a common *vision.*
2. The *structure* of schools should be changed (see Tye, 1987, for
   a discussion of "deep structure" changes).
3. The *culture* of schools should be changed (see Fullan & Miles,
   1992, for a discussion of "reculturing").
4. Attention should be paid to the *philosophies,* values, and
   beliefs that underlie educational practices.
5. *Beliefs* that can result in "second-order" *changes* must be
   addressed, including instructional, societal, and organizational issues (Cuban, 1988) in contrast to mundane issues
   such as discipline and attendance.

In sum, substantially sharing the governance of a school with
empowered teachers is not only drastically different from what

occurs in most schools but also a demanding (and often frightening) undertaking. We wrote this book to share the experiences of successful shared-governance principals. These *individuals* have become experts on democratic schooling and on redesigning schools (see Apple & Beane, 1995; Glickman, in press). And they have much to say that can help principals and teachers alike who are interested in school reform. For the principals who are our subjects, shared governance means that *the fire is back!*

References

Allen, L. (1993). *The role of voice in shared governance: A case study of a primary school.* Unpublished doctoral dissertation, University of Georgia, Athens.

Apple, M. W., & Beane, J. A. (1995). *Democratic schools.* Alexandria, VA: Association for Supervision and Curriculum Development.

Bacharach, S. B., Bamberger, P., Conley, S. C., & Bauer, S. (1990). The dimensionality of decision participation in educational organizations: The value of a multi-domain evaluation approach. *Educational Administration Quarterly, 26,* 126-167.

Bredeson, P. V. (1989). Redefining leadership and the roles of school: Responses to changes in the professional work life of teachers. *High School Journal, 23*(1), 9-20.

Bredeson, P. V. (1994). Empowered teachers—empowered principals: Principals' perceptions of leadership in schools. In N. A. Prestine & P. W. Thurston (Eds.), *Advances in educational administration* (Vol. 3, pp. 195-220). Greenwich, CT: JAI.

Bredeson, P. V. (1995, April). *From gazing out the ivory tower to heavy lifting in the field: Empowerment through collaborative action research.* Paper presented at the annual meeting of the American Educational Research Association, San Francisco.

Calhoun, E. F., & Allen, L. (1994, April). *Results of school wide action research in the league of professional schools.* Paper presented at the annual meeting of the American Educational Research Association, New Orleans, LA.

Chapman, J. D. (1988). Decentralization, devolution and the teacher: Participation by teachers in the decision making of schools. *Journal of Educational Administration, 26*(1), 39-72.

Crockenberg, V., & Clark, W. W. (1979). Teacher participation in school decision making: The San Jose Teacher Involvement Project. *Phi Delta Kappan, 61*(2), 115-118.

Cuban, L. (1988). *The managerial imperative and the practice of leadership in schools.* Albany: State University of New York Press.

Duke, D., Showers, B. K., & Imber, M. (1980). Teachers and shared decision making: The costs and benefits of involvement. *Educational Administration Quarterly, 16*(1), 93-106.

Elmore, R. F. (1993). School decentralization: Who gains? Who loses? In J. Hannaway & M. Carnoy (Eds.), *Decentralization and school improvement* (pp. 33-54). San Francisco: Jossey-Bass.

Fullan, M., & Miles, M. (1992, June). Getting reform right: What works and what doesn't. *Phi Delta Kappan,* 744-752.

Glickman, C. D. (in press). *Education as democracy: The promise of American schools.* San Francisco: Jossey-Bass.

Gutman, A. (1987). *Democratic education.* Princeton, NJ: Princeton University Press.

Halpin, A. W., & Croft, D. B. (1963). *The organizational climate of schools.* Chicago: University of Chicago.

Hawley, W. D. (1988). Missing pieces of the educational reform agenda: Or, why the first and second waves may miss the boat. *Educational Administration Quarterly, 24,* 416-437.

Heck, R. H., Larsen, T. J., & Marcoulides, G. A. (1990). Instructional leadership and school achievement: Validation of a causal model. *Educational Administration Quarterly, 26*(2), 94-125.

King, B., & Kerchner, C. T. (1991, April). *Defining principal leadership in an era of teacher empowerment.* Paper presented at the annual meeting of the American Educational Research Association, Chicago.

Kirby, P.C., & Colbert, R. (1992, April). *Principals who empower teachers.* Paper presented at the annual meeting of the American Educational Research Association, San Francisco.

Kreisberg, S. (1992). *Transforming power: Domination, empowerment, and education.* Albany: State University of New York.

Lightfoot, S. L. (1986). On goodness in schools: Themes of empowerment. *Peabody Journal of Education, 63*(3), 9-28.

Midgley, C., & Wood, S. (1993, November). Beyond site-based management: Empowering teachers to reform schools. *Phi Delta Kappan,* 281-284.

Murphy, J., & Beck, L. G. (in press). *School-based management as school reform: Taking stock.* Thousand Oaks, CA: Corwin.

Neufeld, J., & Freeman, D. (1992, November). *Teachers' perceptions of the principal's role in facilitating teacher empowerment within the ASU-Tempe PDS.* Paper presented at the annual meeting of the Arizona Educational Research Organization, Phoenix, AZ.

Newmann, F. M. (1995). *Successful school restructuring: A report to the public and educators by the Center on Organization and Restructuring.* Madison: University of Wisconsin, Center on Organization and Restructuring.

Nias, J. (1989). *Primary teachers talking.* London: Routledge.

Rallis, S., & Goldring, E. B. (1994, April). *Beyond the individual assessment of principals: School-based accountability in dynamic schools.* Paper presented at the annual meeting of the American Educational Research Association, New Orleans, LA.

Sergiovanni, T. J. (1987). *The principalship: A reflective practice perspective* (2nd ed.). Boston: Allyn & Bacon.

Short, P. M., & Rinehart, J. S. (1992). School participant empowerment scale: Assessment of level of empowerment within the school environment. *Educational and Psychological Measurement, 52*(4), 951-960.

Silins, H. (1994, April). *Leadership characteristics that make a difference to schools.* Paper presented at the annual meeting of the Educational Research Association, New Orleans, LA.

Smith, W. E. (1995, April). *A case study of principal leadership dilemmas in implementing shared decision making.* Paper presented at the annual meeting of the American Educational Research Association, San Francisco.

Tye, B. B. (1987, December). The deep south of schooling. *Phi Delta Kappan,* 245-252.

Weiss, C. (1990, April). *How much shared leadership is there in public high schools?* Paper presented at the annual meeting of the American Educational Research Association, Boston.

2

The Roots of Shared Governance

I just felt the need to have input from everyone. This school is larger than any one person. So, in essence, I just asked them for help in operating this school. I knew it would enhance our school.

—Middle school principal

Experience and research from a variety of school settings often confirm for principals the relevance and efficacy of facilitative/democratic leadership. Other factors that form a powerful impetus for initiating shared governance are educators' philosophy and beliefs, school crises, and professional affiliations. During the initial stages of site-based decision making in Memphis schools, Etheridge and Hall (1991) observed the following patterns of leadership and team development:

1. A *laissez-faire* leadership style did *not* facilitate team development.

2. *Authoritarian* leadership *inhibited* cooperative team functioning. (Principals who had a tendency to monopolize time, control agendas, refuse to share information and decision making, use the vague phrase "We decided," and intimidate others may have actually *provoked* teachers to initiate self-protective action.)

3. *Democratic* leadership was most conducive to a *cooperative team working style* and rapid *group development*. (Predictable but often nerve-racking stages of group development occurred, including membership, subgrouping, confrontation, differentiation, and shared responsibility; see also Bradford & Cohen, 1984, for a detailed explanation of these stages.)

4. *Cooperation with central-office personnel* eased team *progression* toward shared decision making.

5. Except when the principals were democratic leaders, *1 year was insufficient time* for teams to develop into shared decision-making bodies.

6. *Principals often lacked readiness* to implement shared decision making (for example, because of a reluctance to relinquish control, an inability to change, or lack of training).

Several years after the initiation of the Memphis project, Etheridge and Hall (1995) discovered the following patterns:

1. *Democratic* leadership was the only leadership style related to sustained increases in *student achievement*.

2. *Democratic* leadership was *critical* to implementing school-based decision making and to retaining faculty.

3. *Teacher attrition* resulted, in part, from not being allowed to be involved in decision making or from not having principals who were capable of and willing to implement shared decision-making processes.

4. Parental participation was diminished and often eliminated by changing council structures.

5. Lack of program and administrative *continuity* hurt both instruction and student learning.

6. *Student achievement* scores increased in a relatively short time when teachers were empowered or anticipated becoming empowered decision makers.

Such findings can often inform schoolwide change, and as we shall see below, an astute principal can plant and nurture the seeds for such change.

Principal as Initiator

In our study, we found that principals were often the initiators of shared governance in their schools. They commonly "threw the ball out" and got the process started preceding any affiliation with formal shared-governance programs such as the League of Professional Schools. Initiation is difficult, as the principals revealed in our interviews with them. This chapter is about the impetus for involvement in shared-governance initiatives and the difficulties encountered during the early stages of involvement. One principal's story reveals several factors related to these early stages:

> We got into shared governance when I came here because I noticed very low *morale,* a high turnover rate among faculty members, and a large number of "peripheral" [detached, uninvolved] folks. The school was in a huge growth spurt [from 1,200 to 1,800 students], and there was no plan to address it, so people were very frustrated. People needed to give and have their input *valued.* So I met with the whole faculty and was very honest with them about the problems. . . . I had also chatted with groups of people. I told the faculty we needed 10 people to serve on a discipline committee. They said, "Wait a minute—that's always been decided by the principal." But I said, "You need to do it." They gathered data and came up with a student-management plan, which addressed more than just discipline! . . . Then they had other concerns about parking and lunch—nothing but gripes for the first couple years. I hated it, but we just met and hashed out concerns and found solutions. Then I started *sharing the idea of shared governance* with them. I asked, "Why can't you work out your schedules, make curricular decisions, and put your teams together—instead of me doing it? I'm not in the business of telling everybody in June where they are going to be assigned next year!" *Now they select* their own teammates, or teach what they choose to teach. People say, "They're listening to me." *I help them assess* it, *talk* about whether they succeeded, *what* they need to do, and *how* they feel.

Becoming Involved

According to our data, the impetus for involvement in shared governance stems from a variety of sources, including the principal's philosophy; educators' collective beliefs; crises faced by school personnel, parents, and community members; and affiliation in the democratically oriented League of Professional Schools.

The Philosophy of the Principal

Several principals indicated that they had a propensity for shared governance well before they became officially involved in the League of Professional Schools. Many principals considered themselves "participation oriented" at heart: Involvement in the league provided a practical set of guidelines and a structure to formalize and expand their natural inclination.

> *I knew* that if I ever became a principal, *I would empower folks.* Even 12 years ago, when I was an assistant principal, we experimented with things, like giving the MMPI personality test (Minnesota Multiphasic Personality Inventory) to teachers so we could build compatible collaborative teams. . . . We did all kinds of neat stuff, like spreading the word about our restructuring [into a middle school] to all the beauticians and barbershops in town, so the community would get involved in our discussion. When I became a principal, I immediately developed a leadership team. We had gotten $100,000 worth of technological equipment, and I said, "You decide what to do." They just blossomed. They came up with research and development teams, partnerships with business, an invitation to present in California, and a membership in a consortium. I just backed off.

> I've been a principal for 15 years, and I've always had a site-based council, *always.* It's *just the way I operate.* But until we joined the league, I was the chair of the team, I built the agenda, I set up the budget, and I controlled hiring. . . . I can see why, in my early councils, teachers felt they didn't really have any power. Then when the league planned a workshop several years ago, I approached my boss about shared governance. She said no. After the league people talked with her, she relented, but we still had to pay our own dues to join the league. Also, the new superintendent got a mandate from the (school) board to start site-based management. We had already been sharing the governance some, and this would have a snowballing effect. . . . The faculty started doing budget and hiring; they *wanted* to be involved in these things, and they resented the fact that someone was doing the choosing for them, in the case of hiring. Also, I was looking for things I could relinquish to them, and that was the least threatening thing because when teachers help hire their people, they have an interest in seeing them succeed. That was one of our earliest decisions.

We wouldn't have had shared governance if I hadn't said, "Hey, I think this is a better way to run the school." It was the right thing at the right time with the right principal, because I tended to run the school as democratically as people knew how in the 70s. I had no voting structure. I knew there was something better for schools, but *I didn't know exactly what it was.* Then I began to read about Carl Glickman's model of *democratic schooling.* I was ready for a major change, and I knew this was a much better way of running a school. The historical function of American schools is to teach democracy. . . . I put together the right people to go to a league workshop; they were absolutely floating on cloud nine. We got a 98% positive vote to join the league. Carl Glickman, as an expert, was saying the same things I had been saying to the faculty and staff.

One principal's approach to initiating shared governance was unique. It evoked humor among colleagues and also reflected the principal's personal "spark," which can be so motivating to teachers:

I just walked down the hall and asked people, "Do you have a *vision?*" One person said, "When I'm drinking, sometimes I get one." One guy told me he hadn't had one since he was in college in the 60s. I said, "Hang on. I'm serious. Do you have a belief? Can you tell me why you're here?" People said, "Boy, I don't think so." But we need to have a vision! I told the faculty that I'm burning up to do something for these kids, and I'm fired up to do something for the [teaching] folks! So everybody wrote out his or her vision for the school, and we took those little paper bricks and built a foundation. . . . We made a vision team, and a whole bunch of people wanted to be involved in planning and changing this school. We went on a retreat, worked our fannies off, and developed our goals together. We divided into groups. We talked about communication, staff development climate, the biggies. We put study teams together and turned them loose with a lot of data that had been gathered over the years, all we could find. They developed action plans. It just goes on and on.

Educators' Collective Beliefs

The principals whom we interviewed believe that the traditional school organization fails to address the critical need to empower teachers, democratize schooling, improve instruction, and improve the workplace. Initial involvement in shared governance was therefore driven by what many educators—not just principals—believe about quality education and healthy, productive school environments:

> We got involved because we wanted to *truly empower* teachers. . . .
> But even as I am saying empower, I realize you can't empower
> anybody. Teachers must take empowerment upon themselves. We
> just wanted to provide an opportunity for that to happen.

> We didn't get into shared governance just for the sake of involving
> everybody in decision making or for the sake of doing democracy.
> We were really looking at *instructional improvement*. We felt that
> more heads are better than one, and that if we involved a lot of
> people who are close to the students in making decisions about the
> students, then we'd make better decisions.

> We had a reason to bring about change. We knew we were not
> satisfied with the number of kids who were unsuccessful, and we
> felt like those who were successful could be more successful. I had
> seen the shared decision making and team problem-solving ap-
> proach operating at some local plants, and I had heard about
> the league's approach. So I exposed some of the school leaders
> to the idea of empowering teachers and other folks who are closer
> to the kids. Then I kidnapped the teachers and the secretaries and
> the counselors; took them on a daylong retreat. We laid the
> groundwork by seeing tapes and listening to others talk about
> shared governance. . . . A month later, 86% voted to do it.

Crises Faced by School Personnel, Parents, and Community Members

Principals described several occasions when a crisis or problem
provoked interest in the shared-governance approach to schooling.
Ironically, shared governance emphasizes instructional improvement, yet some of the principals and their schools became involved
only after other concerns (*morale problems, discipline problems,* and
significant community changes) had become apparent.

> The impetus to go to shared decision making was that *morale* was
> getting lower and lower. I sensed an element of dissatisfaction
> about what kids were doing and a need for change. We all wanted
> kids to learn more, act better, and be happier, and the teachers
> wanted a better job. My leadership role was to introduce the idea
> of them being part of a democracy, of thinking differently. Having
> a say meant taking responsibility too. Ninety-eight percent buy
> into it now.

We realized *we needed new directions,* we needed to look at ourselves to see what was not right. We had also done a survey that showed concern about parent involvement and discipline. . . . How could we find out why these things were going on, and how could we get a handle on it and then move in the right direction? The principals and a few teachers went to the league's shared governance meeting and brought back the ideas to be discussed in grade-level meetings. We had a 96% positive vote to go forward, partly because we had already been meeting in instructional study groups. But we had to learn about action research and shared decision making.

The community was changing and the school went from 98% white to 78% white. The school was *in a time of crisis* about maintaining high test scores; the teachers were going to have to change the way they were doing things. We needed shared governance to get us through the crisis of the population change with the community. That's when we sent the principals and two teachers to a League meeting.

Affiliation in the League of Professional Schools

Participation in the League of Professional Schools contributed significantly to building interest in and commitment to shared governance. (See Figure 2.1 for general information about the league's structure and foundational beliefs; additional programs with the common purpose of improving student achievement include university-based programs such as Success for All, the Accelerated Schools Project, the School Development Program, and the Coalition of Essential Schools; private enterprises such as the Center for Leadership in School Reform, Effective Schools, and the Teacher Education Institute; and public education projects such as the California School Leadership Academy and the Charter Schools Projects.) Principals explained,

I thought, "We're doing some of this already, in an informal way." I wanted to see how it's being done *around the state,* so I started attending league meetings.

The five people [from our school] who went to the *shared-governance workshops* are very altruistic people who look out for the good of the school. They saw the potential that shared governance has for an organization, and they became really committed to it.

I took a group to the *league meeting* to begin to look at shared governance as a concept and a process. We came back and explained it to the faculty, but they voted not to join the league. That was when I realized that I had to live it, more and more. I couldn't just explain it. Later I pointed out to them how they had given input on the budget and other things—sharing governance without even knowing it. Suddenly people were saying, "This may not be such a bad thing after all." The next year we went to more league meetings.

The representatives who went to find out about shared governance at the league meeting thought it would be great. They then had to get the faculty's input about whether they would be interested. Two *teachers presented* what they learned, and *we voted* unanimously that we wanted to have shared governance.

Frustrations of Initiation

The beginning stages of implementation of shared-governance processes were usually precarious, according to the principals in our study. Principals and teachers were *naive* about many things, including the amount of hard work, the challenge of maintaining an instructional focus, how to include others, and the need to "back off" at the appropriate time.

The Amount of Hard Work

Some principals declared that they had failed to realize that implementing shared governance would be very difficult, although worthwhile:

We found out that shared governance is a lot more than putting names in a hat and electing a leader. We didn't know how difficult it was going to be.

People have found out that democracy isn't all it's cracked up to be, in some ways. *It's work!* And some people would be very comfortable going back to the more traditional approach. . . . Some people enjoy being told what to do; it takes the responsibility off.

The hardest part was for people to realize that they had to be accountable for decisions they made. Suddenly, it wasn't so much fun anymore. They had to become more versed in budget matters

---

The League of Professional Schools: Background

The charter members of the League of Professional Schools began implementing shared governance structures and action research protocols in fall 1990. The league's purpose is to establish representative, democratic decision-making structures to promote teacher involvement in schoolwide instructional and curricular decisions. Governance structures often deal with topics such as staff development, educational materials, program innovation, classroom management, scheduling, budgeting, hiring, and textbook adoption. Action research involves school staff members in collecting, analyzing, and interpreting data to assess the effects of shared decision making on students, teachers, administrators, and parents and to improve decision-making processes and outcomes.

The League of Professional Schools does not specifically prescribe how member schools are to realize their commitment to shared governance. Each school is encouraged to create policies and procedures that fit its unique situation. Membership in the league provides (a) opportunities to network with other schools at periodic meetings involving teams from all league schools; (b) a biannual network exchange newsletter; (c) access to an information-retrieval system to honor requests for information relevant to instructional initiatives; (d) planning, evaluation, research, and instrumentation services via telephone; and (e) a yearly on-site visit by a league staff member, university associate, or league practitioner.

Schools interested in league membership send a team (usually three teachers and the principal) to a two-day orientation and planning workshop in which the central premises of the league—shared governance, action research—are described in the context of instructional and curricular issues. On the basis of this information, staff members of a given school vote (by secret ballot) on becoming league members. An 80% favorable vote is required before schools are eligible to join the league. Using similar voting procedures, each school decides either annually or semiannually whether it wants to continue membership in the league.

Figure 2.1. Background of the League of Professional Schools

(or they'd be left with no money for paper), and they had to think before they made decisions. Regarding the operating budget, it's *their* money, and all I need to hold back is a tiny bit, a tiny chunk to operate the office.

The Challenge of Maintaining
an Instructional Focus

Principals reported that one common problem was the propensity of faculties to address lower-level needs before focusing on instructional and school-improvement matters.

> At the league meeting, they explained how you have to work through Maslow's hierarchy of needs. Teachers had basically said, "If we're going to be empowered, first you're going to make us happy." If you don't *feed* the teachers, they'll *eat* the students. So we *had to address the teachers' basic concerns* before we could do our improvement plan.

> Our first venture in shared governance *didn't go too well*. We needed to prepare a local school plan for improvement, which centered on instruction. But people said the first thing you need to focus on is a parking place for the teacher of the year, and noise in the halls, and hall duty, and other similar things.

> We're still getting too many of the *everyday* concerns. We want to get away from that and get into the big issues like grading, curriculum, promotion, and retention—issues that impact instruction.

Principals responded to the initial challenges of shared governance by limiting the breadth of issues addressed and insisting that faculties maintain a focus on instructional issues, when possible. The following comments of two principals are illustrative:

> That first year, we [principals] really *had to guide* the teachers to keep them talking about instructional things. We asked, "What is bothering you about student learning?" They said we needed more at-risk programs, and we needed a foreign language program—and if we began to talk about something like parking, we sent it back to the liaison group. Then we got their input and summarized it into five instructional goals. Then when we took it to the leadership council, they wanted to approve it in a hurry and then spend a lot of time talking about parking and bathrooms and things like that!

> There was a lot of griping in liaison groups during the first couple of years. We *had to limit* it to one priority concern from each group when the executive council met. It was good, though, because we could then improve things or explain them, at least. We were listening! For example, teachers were upset about interruptions for delivering lunches the kids had forgotten, and we set up a good policy and procedure to deal with that.

In Chapter 7, we discuss *focus* more fully.

The Importance of Inclusion

Principals also reported that taking special care in selection, rotation, and inclusion of persons on school councils, liaison groups, and task forces paid great dividends.

> Everybody put his or her name on a piece of paper and put it in a hat. I put group numbers—1, 2, 3, 4, 5, 6—on the overhead, and we pulled out names to divide up into groups. If a group has two sixth-grade teachers or two cafeteria workers, we move one to the next group. Then *each group elected a person* to represent them on the executive council.
>
> We decided *we had to include* grade-level chairpersons, the exploratories, and special education on the leadership council as well as the elected persons, because they're real important to certain decisions.
>
> We decided on *regular rotation* of leadership of liaison groups. At first you were just elected to stay on forever, but after a few years some of them just weren't that involved anymore. They had liked being elected to "represent the union" or to get their two cents in. . . . Maybe they were disillusioned. So we now have a rotation of 2-year terms.
>
> We had a super *task force* that changed our whole grading procedure and report cards. It all went through task forces, liaison groups, leadership council, the executive council, and the entire faculty before we presented it to the board of education. It was drastic, and we made many changes with lots of grumbling, but it's working. Now if a student fails in a class, the child and his or her parent can request a "contract for success" to change the U (we don't use F's anymore) to a higher grade.

In Chapter 5, we discuss the inclusion of parents and students in shared-governance schools.

The Need to Back Off

As they worked with teachers to initiate shared-governance processes, principals came to realize how their role had changed. Most of the principals learned how to back off and allow a school democracy to develop.

I definitely have less power than before. In some ways, I'd say I have less power than the teachers. [Teachers] will listen to an administrator with a global viewpoint, but they *defer to what the other teachers believe* is best because they're in the classrooms.

The teachers were frustrated after they had constructed a discipline program, and those people who didn't want to do it, didn't. They wanted me to write letters calling those people to task, *but I'm no longer going to be out there hitting people over the head* with a hard rock. *This is the government of shared implementation, not the government of fear.* They have also had to realize that when they select personnel, they will be living with them. They can't blame the principal. I'm still the principal, and I'm still the only person who has the authority to reprimand someone, even though usually the faculty encourages those people to move on, and they do.

It's one of those things. If I come before the faculty and say, "This is something I want," then *99.9% of the time they follow,* even though they know they have the right to dissent and some of them don't particularly care for the way it's going. *I don't want this anymore.*

I decided *I really shouldn't be running* the leadership council meetings. The teachers were looking for my reaction to things; they were afraid if they didn't vote the same way I did, it would be held against them. So *we got a teacher leader* for the committee. It is symbolic, partly, and the teachers feel more empowered. It has worked really well.

A real difference now is that *I have stopped selecting* faculty, students, and parents for the leadership team. It used to be like the president's Cabinet, but now we have a representative democracy instead of me just selecting. It's made a world of difference.

At the same time, at least one principal remained partially stuck—perhaps temporarily—in old patterns:

I'm not sure it's really in keeping with democratic ideas, but *I appoint* the grade-level chairpersons. Because they have a vote on the leadership council, they should probably be elected, according to the league's philosophy. They are kind of like the House of Lords, and generally their allegiance is to their grade level, not the whole school.

In Chapter 3, we further discuss "backing off."

Results

Becoming involved in a shared-governance initiative is a challenge that requires hard work, staying the course, including others, and backing off. It is also about "muddling through," trial and error, and experimenting. Sometimes it even requires a bit of politicking. Despite its difficulties, the principals in our study *reveled* in the deep commitment, the trust, and the significant opportunities for collaboration that shared governance afforded. Clearly, these factors helped to build a healthy and productive school environment:

> We believe in what's best for the kids. . . . If we ever disagree about an issue, *we show a unified front*. It may seem hard or cold, but when I interview [a teacher] I say, "There's no middle ground with me; either you're on board or you're not."

> With the shift in responsibility *we now share the credit, and we share the fault*. It's a real give and take, on a real equal basis. The teachers know they have a say and that they can outvote me. There's an element of trust.

> I've *sent folks out to other schools* to look at their shared-governance models—models that work a little or a lot better than ours.

One of the finest testimonials to the success of shared governance vis-à-vis the teachers' experience came from a middle school principal:

> When my predecessor left, the faculty wrote a letter to the school board demanding another shared-governance principal. It had become part of the school's culture that teachers make decisions; *the faculty would mutiny if an autocratic principal came in!*

Unfortunately, however, such experiences stand in sharp contrast to the all-too-typical ways that shared governance is initiated. In fact, one of the principals in our study was initially *directed* by the central office to establish shared governance:

> The Board of Education *mandated*, through the new superintendent, that we start site-based management.

In cases such as this, the potential for mutual growth, inclusion, and educational improvement in a school embarking on a shared-governance initiative is undermined by orders that contradict a foundational principle of shared governance: choice.

In the next chapter, we discuss the challenge of developing virtuosity in school leadership.

References

Bradford, D. L., & Cohen, A. R. (1984). *Managing for excellence*. New York: John Wiley.

Etheridge, C. P., & Hall, M. L. A. (1991, April). *The nature, role and effect of competition, cooperation, and comprehension: Multiple site implementation of SBDM*. Paper presented at the annual meeting of the American Educational Research Association, Chicago.

Etheridge, C. P., & Hall, M. L. A. (1995, April). *Challenge to change: The Memphis experience with school-based decision making revisited*. Paper presented at the annual meeting of the American Educational Research Association, San Francisco.

3

Virtuosity in Leadership

Becoming an "Unleader"

Essentially, these people are being asked to modify their per-
sonalities.

—Conley (1993, p. 83)

Shared governance has given me the opportunity to grow and to see
teachers come alive. It's exciting to see teachers start to realize what's
been suppressed in them for years, because of dominating and
self-centered principals. Suddenly, what motivated them at the start
of their careers comes back. I've had people say, "I was going to quit,
but now I'm so excited about being here." It's good stuff. It works.

—Middle school principal

Principals are facing more role changes than any other group
involved in school reform (Bradley, 1992). Murphy (1994) describes the changing nature of the principal's role in terms of several
patterns:

- ◆ Leading from the center
- ◆ Enabling and supporting teacher success
- ◆ Managing reform
- ◆ Extending the school community

Many principals have faced these radical role changes and other changes—for example, the role's current ambiguity (Prestine, 1991a)—with courage and determination. Our study indicates that shared-governance principals frame their new role in new *beliefs,* enact it through five primary *strategies,* and achieve (or approximate) what we call *virtuosity in leadership.* This chapter briefly describes these beliefs, strategies, and experiences to set the stage for a more detailed discussion of principals' development in succeeding chapters.

New Beliefs

Successful shared-governance principals believe in backing off, facilitating the work of others, and building an inclusive school community.

Backing Off

The hallmark of shared-governance leadership is a principal who supports and affirms teacher leadership (Clift, Johnson, Holland, & Veal, 1992). Prestine (1991b) found that shared-governance principals develop the ability to "read" and "interpret" situations while empowering others and maintaining a leadership presence. Murphy (1992) calls this process "orchestrating from the sidelines." According to Macpherson (1989), "Principals have to . . . allow part of their professional self to die and be bereaved . . . and then negotiate a new and dimly perceived future in the emerging organizations" (p. 42).

Bredeson (1991) compares this aspect of leadership to the process of recognizing the dysfunctional features of a role, *letting go* of elements impeding change, and negotiating more satisfying roles to replace old roles. This may be easier said than done in light of the need to vary one's approach to empowering leadership in response to contextual changes. To illustrate, Peterson and Solsrud (1993) found that principals are important to restructuring efforts as initiators, facilitators, cheerleaders, visionaries, and managers, but they become less necessary to those efforts as teachers become increasingly involved in school leadership. In particular, the principals who participated in our study emphasized the importance of "backing off" or "letting go":

> It's a lot of give and take—knowing when to assert yourself and *when to sit back and allow others* to take charge. You balance things, and each situation is different.

> I am more involved now than I have ever been, although *I backed away* from the shared-governance committee decisions because I didn't want to unduly influence teachers by my presence.

> I've gotten a lot better at knowing when to *keep my mouth shut.* I still need to work on it, but I'm better. Now I pretty much think I can live with anything as long as it's legal, ethical, and moral.

> It requires me to deal with more people than I used to, and I have to *be a better listener.* Sometimes I *have to back off* and let others' views come into play . . . and then let the chips fall.

> I never say, "This will be a school where each and every teacher will use the whole language philosophy." *I'm not going to force* teachers who are uncomfortable to use that strategy.

> *I try not to give a lot of my own input* because I want things to be teacher initiated.

> I *do not sit in* any of the grade-level meetings because when an administrator is around, teachers tend to go with the administrator.

> Sometimes I feel very much like *I'm just another participant.*

We note, however, that even a principal who works hard at backing off must occasionally "step in":

> If you're a shared-governance principal, you've got to be mature enough *to know when to step in,* when shared governance won't work to resolve an issue. Sometimes groups of people won't do something or can't come together. You have to monitor things, which takes guts, but you have to do it.

Overall, our research suggests that backing off, or letting go, requires that principals

- ◆ *extract* themselves from decision-making processes to a great extent
- ◆ *avoid* monitoring teachers and contradicting their decisions

- encourage teachers to participate voluntarily in committee and task force work
- move to elect executive council members (rather than personally appoint them)
- *encourage* teachers to represent the school at regional meetings of shared-governance schools
- make *few* unilateral decisions
- *"let go,* and let the chips fall" (that is, be open to risk and experimentation)
- *reconcile* within themselves the erroneous but inevitable perception of some that a leader who backs off is weak

Actions such as these give teachers the opportunity to share power, make decisions, and take responsibility for their decisions. These actions also reduce the chances that teachers will second-guess or sabotage decisions that principals are required to make.

Facilitating the Work of Others

"The principal of a successful school is not the instructional leader but the coordinator of teachers as instructional leaders" (Glickman, 1991, p. 7).

Aronstein, Marlow, and Desilets (1990) note that principals must shift from being decision makers to being *facilitators*. Goldman, Dunlap, and Conley (1993) indicate that being a successful facilitator requires the following:

- Acquiring and arranging *resources* that support activities and aspirations
- Grouping people who can work well together and who collectively possess the necessary skills to complete designated tasks
- Providing *feedback* and *reinforcement*
- Providing *links* between the school and the community
- Collecting and distributing *information* that allows teachers to have more control over work conditions and teaching methods
- Allowing broad *participation* in decision making

- Lobbying for movement toward *goals* instead of exercising formal authority in meetings
- Becoming a role *model* of the school's vision
- Helping others accept the idea that externally imposed, bureaucratic regulations preclude independent operation of a school *and* that a bottom-up system of participative decision making is a *counterbalance* (as opposed to an alternative) to the top-down exercise of power
- Building *cooperation* between school and central-office personnel to achieve goals that are mutually acceptable

We found that the shared-governance principals in our study increasingly use *facilitative power* (working *with* rather than *over* others) as an alternative to authoritarian forms of power. In essence, these principals help others achieve goals that are shared, negotiated, and complementary (Dunlap & Goldman, 1991).

> My new role is facilitator. In my old role I was decision maker, supervisor, evaluator . . . and lonely. That sounds funny, but I really was. Because of your position of power, you are automatically separated from the faculty. You have all the authority and all the responsibility. I'll tell you that it was a much more defined and simple concept; you don't spend a lot of time questioning where you fit into the puzzle. Two years ago I was crying on everybody's shoulder; I thought, "Now that they've got power, they don't need me anymore." We had to work through where everybody fit in, including me.

> I have become more of a *facilitator of other leaders,* and it's much more demanding.

> I try to be *a resource and a facilitator.* It's tough to get folks away from always looking to the principal.

> I am now *a resource person and a facilitator.* Teachers feel they are my equal, and they do whatever they really want to do. But they are also accountable; what's done is logical and makes sense for kids—it can't be some wacko thing. So my role is to listen, to encourage teachers, to talk with them, to help them see what the results of their efforts are.

> It requires more leadership skill. It's not an issue of my power; I don't go in and tell them, "This is what you need to be doing." It's more like, *"How can I help you* do what's going to be done?"

Indeed, facilitation takes many forms among the principals we studied, including support of programs as well as support of shared-governance processes. Principals facilitated educators' work by

- providing planning *time*
- assisting in the development of a common *vision*
- arranging *group* development activities
- accessing and providing *information and data* for decision making
- providing professional *literature*
- helping teachers learn about *action research* (see, for example, Calhoun, 1994)
- providing *money* for teachers to attend shared-governance workshops

In fact, our data suggest that principals are the *primary* force in attaining conditions in the school that allow restructuring to occur. Not surprisingly, this finding is consistent with the work of other researchers (e.g., Prestine, 1991a). *Facilitative principals* use understanding and skill to turn change processes over to teachers and others; part of this work includes a commitment to changing the school and an ability to build early commitments in others, often by introducing and clarifying the concept of shared governance and by creating a sense of urgency for school change through active involvement, modeling, and "courtship" (Chenoweth & Kushman, 1993). In essence, shared-governance principals lead others to lead themselves. Manz and Sims (1984) call such principals "unleaders"; their work is characterized by

- effective and efficient goal accomplishment
- self-renewal
- free and open communication
- trust among its members
- shared leadership
- ownership
- division of labor
- positive norms

Building a More Inclusive School Community

An impressive body of research now shows that redesigned schools tend to "blend" with their communities, so that over time the boundaries between these schools and their communities become "more permeable" (Goldring & Rallis, 1992, p. 3). This requires principals to promote the school in the community and to be sensitive to parents and other people in the community (as well as to students and staff). We and others (e.g., Earley, Baker, & Weindling, 1990) have found that the public relations role consumes more and more of the principals' time:

> Everything I do is related in some way to the *community's expectations* and what needs to be done in the school.

> On some things there's less work—like the curriculum work. But then there's more in other areas. And it takes more time to make decisions when you have a *lot of people*—including parents and other citizens—involved in it.

Although spending numerous hours interacting with others can be stressful (and lack of time is change's worst enemy), the principals we studied readily acknowledged the advantages of having available the skills of diverse people as well as sharing the complex responsibilities of serving the students:

> *Everybody has something to offer,* and everybody is equally important. And I understand that I don't have all the answers.

> The whole thing is about what's in the best interest of the students; for that, we have to have *input from a lot of different people.* And we have to educate those people about making decisions and giving input.

In Chapter 5, we discuss inclusion of parents and students in more detail.

Five Key Strategies That Support
Shared Governance

The principals we interviewed exhibited five primary strategies for supporting and achieving shared governance in their schools.

With only a few clues as to how to operate in accord with the principles of shared governance, all of these educators realized through trial and error that restructuring a school for democratic decision making requires *trust, openness, effective communication and sharing of information, consensus and accountability,* and a *willingness to embrace inevitable and healthy conflict.*

Building Trust

Recent studies have emphasized the importance of developing a *relationship of trust* between teachers and the principal in restructured schools (Smylie, 1992). Shared-governance principals say this is a central aspect of the role changes required of them and includes *modeling trust* and *respecting others:*

> The key to becoming a shared-governance school is to have the focus on the administrator initially. The folks see that person *living his or her belief in shared governance,* and they learn trust in shared governance.

> Your role changes, and you have to be able to think differently. You've got to *trust* people to do the right thing, and you've got to have *patience.* It's risky, and it may not work.

> I think you have to like people. You have to *think of teachers as equals to you,* and not as people who work for you. You're working with them a lot more closely, and you're not going to just tell them what to do.

Genuine delegation of responsibility and shared power emerge from this reciprocal relationship of trust. Trust also replaces formal authority, as shared-governance principals explained:

> I see myself getting *more input* from teachers. And, if I ask them for input, I'm honestly and truthfully going to use it. One of the keys to shared governance is getting teachers to trust you.

> My response to teachers is to say, "Whatever you can do, I want you to do it." They tell people that their principal gives them the *opportunity to do* basically what they know they need to do as teachers.

> The level of trust between me and the teachers is much higher. The decisions are better ones, too. I would never do it any other way now.

Shared-governance principals are also likely to extend responsibility and authority to assistant principals, a tacit demonstration of trust:

> I was an assistant principal for 1 year, and the only thing I did was discipline. I had no sense of what the principalship was about. When I became a principal, I gave the assistants a lot of responsibility. The only responsibility they didn't have was signing the checks.

For more about trust, see Chapter 2 of our book *Empowering Teachers* (Blase & Blase, 1994).

Modeling Openness

Shared-governance principals establish openness in a variety of ways. They do so by *listening,* by actively encouraging *input* and *feedback* (including *criticism* of self and programs), and by making themselves *available* for interaction and discussion:

> Before shared governance, I just made the decisions. I did what I thought was best. I chose staff development from what I saw in other schools, what I thought the teachers should do. Now I've *learned to listen more* and to see where teachers are. Instead of saying, "Everybody must go," the teachers themselves are choosing to go to workshops to strengthen themselves.

> I'm *giving teachers the opportunity* to say, "These are some of the things I'm truly having problems with."

> We're constantly *talking,* looking at things we can do to improve.

Establishing Effective Communication and Sharing Information

An essential element in shared-governance principals' approach to leadership is *establishing effective communication:*

> I *draw so much on my ability to communicate,* verbally and nonverbally.

> Now I have to be very astute, have very good interpersonal skills. I can't just put people down for suggesting things that just won't work. I can't just say, "Tom, we can't suspend people every time they

get sent to the office." I have to say, "Let's do some investigating, find out the parameters, and find out why there are rules," or else Tom gets real offended. . . . Sometimes people start arguing with each other, and they start taking it personally, so interpersonal skills like communication, conflict resolution, problem solving, and decision making with others is by far number one.

Every year *I share* my personal goals (which are aligned, in part, with the school goals but which are solely about *me*) with the staff. *I ask* everybody for recommendations on how to achieve these goals. I ask if I accomplished last year's goals and *I get input.* Then I send out another document saying, "Here are my personal goals as a result of your input." This year *they told me,* "You need to slow down and listen, even though you are busy and the demands on you are great." They also told me, "We'd like to see you in a presentation role more; we'd like for you to teach us." That was a real compliment, and *I did it.*

I graduated from this school. When I came back as principal, I heard that people have a perception that this school is a dump, and I took exception to that. I wanted people working here to have the same level of commitment that I have to the school. So I've been perceived as a very dominating principal in the past, but I've always tried—maybe not successfully enough—to *have input from the teachers.*

I have to *be open* and flexible. It requires constant reflection.

Shared-governance principals perceive that teachers are more willing to share decision-making responsibilities in an open, collaborative, facilitative, and supportive atmosphere than in a closed and controlling one (Smylie, 1992). Our research indicates that openness and encouragement extend even to matters such as teacher evaluation:

Our form of teacher evaluation is a positive look at what they are doing; it offers them an opportunity to improve and to review what they are about. We encourage the teachers, pat them on the back, and we work with them if there are problems. In the past it's been "Do we keep or get rid of this one?"

Conger and Kanungo (1988) suggest that leaders should provide viable *opportunities* for people in organizations to gain *knowledge* and skills to improve their work. The principals in our study vigorously facilitated teacher decision making by helping teachers get needed *information,* a point consistent with findings produced by Goldman, Dunlap, and Conley (1991). Such information may concern restructuring, technical matters, personnel, budget, instruction, or implementation of reforms (Conley, 1991; Prestine, 1991b). Shared-governance principals are aware of the important link between access to knowledge and successful teacher empowerment. This latter point is also emphasized in the work of Kirby and Colbert (1992). The principals we interviewed remarked,

> I try to tell the staff as much as possible. They're more well-versed, and I think they should be. When I go to a meeting, I learn something, and I also try to share with them. I'm not an overseer at any meeting.

> I feel a real responsibility to give information, to inform the staff about research articles as well as administrivia.

In fact, information and professional knowledge are such important factors that they form the basis of some approaches to school restructuring. Lichtenstein, McLaughlin, and Knudsen (1991) found that most reform initiatives that stressed decentralization and enhanced authority for teachers were so poorly conceived and implemented that they had little effect on teacher empowerment. However, these researchers found that *professional knowledge* could be a solid foundation for teacher empowerment. Broadly conceived, professional knowledge includes knowledge of the professional community of teachers, which helps teachers recognize their own and others' expertise as well as what is possible; knowledge of and participation in education policy at local, state, and national levels; and knowledge of subject area, which is the foundation of their authority, the basis for involvement, and a relevant factor in policy decisions. Lichtenstein et al. cite some of the benefits of knowledge-based reforms:

> After a year of examining structural, formal, and institution-based efforts to empower teachers, we shifted our research to look at knowledge-based reforms. This approach did indeed lead us to teachers who believe they are fundamentally empowered in principle and practice, whose attitudes about teaching are upbeat and hopeful—in many cases enthusiastic—and who believe that their practice represents a model of professionalism that ought to be widely developed. In addition, we saw that *knowledge carries its own authority*. We met teachers working in "unreconstructed" or "nonrestructured" settings who reported that

they were revitalized—professionally empowered—through *access to professionally relevant knowledge.* (p. 3)

(For ideas about encouraging openness and establishing effective communication, see Blase & Blase, 1994.)

Achieving Consensus and Personal Accountability

The process by which educators in shared-governance schools achieve consensus is apparently highly variable within the same school and across schools. Consensus seems to occur most often in planned discussions among *all* people who have interests in the issue. On occasion, individuals remind the group that a particular issue that should be *jointly* resolved has yet to be discussed by the entire group. One thing is clear, however, people in shared-governance schools assiduously attempt to *avoid* voting on issues; they want to reduce the chances of creating "winners" and "losers" in group decisions. Particularly helpful in this regard are mutual respect gained through active listening and a serious examination of all contributions. We found that the principal's primary tasks in achieving consensus are *encouraging discussion* and *participating as an equal.* Regarding the latter, principals stated,

> I'm a member of the instructional committee, but I'm considered ex officio. I really have no power. They meet, they discuss, and they reach consensus. We don't tally votes. *We just ask, "Do we all agree?"*

> I remember what it felt like to be a teacher and work for a dictator. I didn't like it at all, the fact that somebody was telling me what I had to do and how I had to do it. As a principal, *there are very few decisions I make unilaterally.* If I ever do, somebody reminds me, "We didn't discuss that."

However, principals disclosed that unsuccessful decisions reached through consensus were sometimes disowned by the decision makers:

> When the teachers started doing something they had agreed on but it failed, they ran away like little rats! . . . I look like a Benedict Arnold when I remind them that we all agreed to this. Then I wonder whether consensus had really been reached. I heard so much griping I thought they might *go back to the old way.*

In such cases, principals may not only reflect on whether decision-making processes are truly based on consensus but also struggle with the *accountability dilemma*. This dilemma has been described by Hallinger, Murphy, and Hausman (1992) as centering on principals' belief that if parents and teachers share decision-making authority, they should also be held accountable for decisions. Even in the schools we studied, empowering others did not negate the fact that, ultimately, the principal is *officially and legally accountable*:

> The only thing that really hasn't changed is that *I am still ultimately accountable* for every function of the school . . . budget, personnel.

> I still feel that *the buck stops at my desk,* though. Absolutely, positively. I feel accountable for many things, but not everything. Maybe I'm a watchdog.

Indeed, shared-governance principals continue to struggle with the legitimate and reasonable act of "giving away" or sharing authority.

> It's hard because *I feel a little like I have all the responsibility but not much authority,* whereas in the old system I was in charge. But I gave that authority away on purpose. I still feel accountable for things, whether they fail or are successful.

Some shared-governance principals rescind such authority only in exigent circumstances:

> There are some things you can't take before the committee because it might mean that a decision is made 2 or 3 weeks late. You *can't wait* for that, so there are times when you have to make decisions.

Other principals are seemingly unable to fully empower teachers under any circumstances:

> OK, I'm a benevolent dictator. I allow my people to do a lot of things, but when it comes down to running this school, everybody in this town knows *who's in charge* and who's accountable to the superintendent. There's no question.

In our opinion, principals exhibiting the healthiest attitudes about the issue of accountability in shared-governance schools consider *themselves* accountable to others in the decision-making process and demonstrate this, in part, by their openness to feedback on their performance.

> Now *I'm accountable* to the staff. In the old days, I could do something, and they might grumble and bluster and carry on, but they wouldn't dare say anything for fear of being written up. Now, I hear feedback all the time about myself, plus I do a parent/community/staff survey of my leadership every year.

Again, we see that true shared governance requires that principals redesign their roles and responsibilities. In studies of the Chicago schools, Smylie and Crowson (1993) found that new governing structures frequently placed principals in ambiguous and potentially precarious positions regarding authority and responsibility.

> Implicitly, there were expectations that principals would try to help, not hinder or sabotage, these new decision-making structures. They were expected to adapt their workaday activities to accommodate the processes of shared decision making. They were also expected to participate actively as members of new decision-making bodies. Implicitly, it was also expected that principals who were unable or unwilling to adapt would leave the district. Indeed, some have elected to do so. (p. 73)

Smylie and Crowson explained that in Chicago scant attention was paid to the new role of the principal; it was not determined *a priori* which decisions remained the prerogative of the principal or which were the responsibilities of the teachers. Furthermore, Chicago principals faced a dilemma that pitted their *facilitative* role against their *accountability* to ensure decision compliance. Invoking traditional hierarchical control over teachers risked violating newly established collaborative processes. But these principals also thought that they were under scrutiny to make reform a reality, and they were uncomfortable with added accountability amid reduced control.

Embracing Conflict

Peterson and Solsrud (1993) and Terry (1993) have found that the redistribution of power during restructuring efforts fosters greater faculty commitment to the school but may also foster greater conflict. Rinehart, Short, and Johnson (1994) observed a positive relationship between faculty empowerment and conflict because the conflict arises out of an open disclosure of values and beliefs.

The shared-governance principals we interviewed are acutely aware of the potential benefits of conflict. They understand that conflict is a normal part of group development and is often a healthy aspect of problem solving, although this may seem contradictory (Glickman, 1990). (Conflict is addressed further in Chapter 4.)

Principals in our study reported that as openness and expressiveness among faculty and staff increased, *productive forms of conflict* (e.g., disagreement, debate)—conflict without personal hostility—frequently resulted. In response, principals

- ◆ did *not* attempt to *suppress* conflict
- ◆ highlighted the *productive aspects* of conflict
- ◆ found ways to *reduce* unproductive conflict
- ◆ emphasized mutual *respect*
- ◆ *educated* teachers about conflict

Given the inevitability of conflict, League of Professional Schools consultants routinely educate teachers about it, often in the context of addressing issues related to group development. In their work, league consultants and principals often use a description of the stages of group development with teachers (e.g., Stanford & Roark, 1974; see Figure 3.1.)

Consequently, conflict is usually viewed as a *positive force* in shared-governance deliberations:

> There's conflict, but it's *good conflict.* If a person really does not agree, then that person says so. You know where the other person's coming from.

> There's a different kind of frustration now. We have a lot of conflict now because people feel strongly about the things they do. Our consultant reminded us that *people without vision never get*

frustrated because they never have the opportunity for conflict. It used to be that people either complained in the lounge or just had a good time having coffee together. Now people are talking about instruction, discipline, grading, and asking what others think about it. There's *more conflict,* but when the changes work, things are a lot better.

An account of tactics that principals use to manage conflict can be found in Schmuck and Runkel (1994).

Virtuosity in Leadership

Successful shared-governance leadership requires *virtuosity in leadership*—a principal must sharpen the focus on instruction while encouraging teachers' growth and tapping their talents.

Sharpening the Focus on Instruction

Contrary to the experience of some principals involved in school reform (e.g., Weindling, 1992), the principals (and schools) that we studied were moving toward, not away from, a focus on instruction. Shared-governance principals devote more, not less, time to instructional leadership, and they seem to enjoy it:

Several things are different. Number one, I spend a great deal more time *discussing instruction* with teachers and less time doing some other traditional administrative things. This is good; it's what a principal ought to be doing. Bureaucracies tend to generate unimportant things, a lot of paperwork that's not very necessary.

I spend time going to conferences and meetings that *focus on instruction* instead of administration. It has changed the nature of my work, and it has changed how I learn professionally. I couldn't tell you the last time I went to the state principals' meeting. I used to go faithfully, but too much time is spent at those meetings on administrative issues. Now I spend my time learning about cooperative learning, instructional strategies, or shared governance.

We discuss the maintenance of an instructional focus in Chapter 7.

Figure 3.1. Stages in group development.

	Interaction Pattern	Process and Focus	Communication
Stage 1: Beginning	Randomness or leader centered Pairing and subgrouping	Confusion Searching Protective & seeking allies	Guarded Constricted Topic and situation centered
Stage 2: Norm development	Erratic, tentative Usually leader centered or leader directed	Testing limits Seeking answers Trial balloons, leadership tests	Security oriented Situation centered Little self-disclosure
Stage 3: Conflict distorted	Erratic; centers on one person, pair, or both, depending on issue; or random.	Confrontive Hostile labeling Anxious Conflict	One-way distorted labeling Some self-disclosure, usually in anger or retaliation
Stage 4: Transition	Less erratic Patterns develop Less centered on leader	Vacillate between task and group concerns Focus on new norms and personal feelings	Self-disclosure and feedback More open and less labeling
Stage 5: Productive	Interaction pattern based on task at hand	Cooperation Group leadership Group is a group, *we* purpose	Open, within limits of disclosure Feedback and intimacy norms
Stage 6: Affection	Group-centered but moving to individual in focus	I-Thou interaction often Intimacy norms changed to more intimacy	More self-disclosure and risk Positive feedback
Stage 7: Actualizing	Pattern appropriate to task Usually group centered	Flexible—move from task to person to group as appropriate	Open, constructive, accurate; based on being rather than need

SOURCE: Adapted, with permission, from *Human Interaction in Education*, by G. Stanford and A. E. Roark, 1974, Boston: Allyn & Bacon.

Encouraging Teachers' Growth and Tapping Their Talents

Principals' support of teachers' growth goes hand in hand with developing a sharp focus on instruction. Principals delight in empowering teachers, and they work vigorously to tap teachers' special talents:

> I have a whole new vision about leadership. It's helped me to grow, it's opened more doors, it's more inclusive. There are *more leaders,* more sharing, more shared responsibility. *It's not as lonely* because everybody is included in the power base. It's so much fun to watch people grow as leaders; some have emerged as excellent leaders. It's wonderful.

> I spend time trying to *find ways to empower teachers.* I want them to be more empowered than they want to be; I'm ahead of them on that. Still, they don't yet want to be making tough decisions like evaluating department heads.

In fact, shared-governance principals often fade into the background themselves, minimize limits to teacher decision making and action, and push gently for teacher leadership:

> I just have to implement things like the broad time frame for our schedule and teacher sick leave, and other policy things. But beyond that, *the teachers can take things and turn them* any way they wish.

> Teachers are now allowed to *do as much as they are able* to do, and the limits are very few.

> I suggested that *they handle the total budget,* but some of them don't like it because with that comes responsibility. Nonetheless, after discussion I said, "We'll give it a shot." They worked out the process for all teachers to be involved in the budget.

> One time we needed a chairperson for a group, and I said, *"I'm not here."* I picked up my briefcase and walked out, saying, "Now you're on your own." Well, one of the folks emerged as the chairperson, and now the committee has goals, plans, and a budget.

> I still have to evaluate people, but you'd be surprised how *teachers are policing their problems* in this new climate. A couple weeks ago, a group of teachers wanted me to go in and tell a fellow member of their group that she wasn't doing this and that. I said, "She's your team member."

It's not that you have to be *manipulative* when you give teachers opportunities to *learn leadership skills*. Actually, you have to be open and honest, and you have to believe in democracy. My philosophy has always been that schools should be more *democratic* than they were when I was raised.

Now it's more important for me to go with the teachers to league meetings. I need to help teachers stay trained in how to make decisions, *how to be leaders*. I give them more professional training opportunities so they can develop their leadership skills.

You've got to be able to read people. You've got to listen. You've got to study the concept of shared governance. . . . You don't spend money on a discipline package, for example, when you've got very knowledgeable teachers right here. They know every trick in the book, and with some leadership and a chance to get together, *they can do the program* themselves.

A Word of Caution: Principal as the Target of Influence

Prestine (1991b) learned that principals in restructured schools are often seen by both parents and teachers as "targets of influence." Such people often request principals to make unilateral decisions on their behalf. Consequently, principals may have difficulty surrendering power to and sharing power with teachers and others. Traditional norms, routines, and expectations reinforce the role of principal as decision maker. The shared-governance principals we talked to alluded to related difficulties:

In this part of the state, the principal is the *lightning rod*. Nobody would come in and say, "I would like to talk to the Committee for School Improvement chairman." Instead, it's "I want to talk to the principal." That has to be balanced; we have to get to the point where people understand that this is how we govern ourselves.

I'm still in the role whereby if the staff doesn't follow what the leadership team decides, *the leadership team wants me to enforce it*.

Successful shared-governance principals learn to use the influence of others to fulfill their own facilitative role. In doing this, these principals avoid sabotaging shared-governance efforts:

I allow people to *talk to me, to advise, to experience different things.* It makes the school better because I'm getting it from all sides and can share thinking across groups.

References

Aronstein, L. W., Marlow, M., & Desilets, B. (1990). Detours on the road to site-based management. *Educational Leadership, 47*(7), 28-31.

Blase, J., & Blase, J. R. (1994). *Empowering teachers: What successful principals do.* Thousand Oaks, CA: Corwin.

Bradley, A. (1992). New study laments lack of change in Chicago classrooms. *Education Week, 11*(27), 1, 19.

Bredeson, P. V. (1991, April). *Letting go of outlived professional identities: A study of role transition for principals in restructured schools.* Paper presented at the annual meeting of the American Educational Research Association, Chicago.

Calhoun, E. (1994). *How to use action research in the self-renewing school.* Alexandria, VA: Association for Supervision and Curriculum Development.

Chenoweth, T., & Kushman, J. (1993, April). *Courtship and school restructuring: Building early commitment to school change for at-risk schools.* Paper presented at the annual meeting of the American Educational Research Association, Atlanta, GA.

Clift, R., Johnson, M., Holland, P., & Veal, M. L. (1992). Developing the potential for collaborative school leadership. *American Educational Research Journal, 29*(4), 877-908.

Conger, J. A., & Kanungo, R. N. (1988). The empowerment process: Integrating theory and practice. *Academy of Management Review, 13*(3), 471-482.

Conley, D. T. (1991). Lessons from laboratories in school restructuring and site-based decision making. *Oregon School Study Council Bulletin, 34*(7), 1-61.

Conley, D. T. (1993). *Road map to restructuring.* Eugene: University of Oregon, ERIC Clearinghouse on Educational Management.

Dunlap, D., & Goldman, P. (1991). Rethinking power in schools. *Educational Administration Quarterly, 27*(1), 5-29.

Earley, P., Baker, L., & Weindling, D. (1990). *"Keeping the raft afloat": Secondary headship five years on.* London: National Foundation for Educational Research in England and Wales.

Glickman, C. D. (1990). Pushing school reform to a new edge: The seven ironies of empowerment. *Phi Delta Kappan, 72*(1), 68-75.

Glickman, C. D. (1991). Pretending not to know what we know. *Educational Leadership, 48*(8), 4-10.

Goldman, P., Dunlap, D. M., & Conley, D. T. (1991, April). *Administrative facilitation and site-based school reform project.* Paper presented at the annual meeting of the American Educational Research Association, Chicago.

Goldman, P., Dunlap, D. M., & Conley, D. T. (1993). Facilitative power and nonstandardized solutions to school site restructuring. *Educational Administration Quarterly, 29*(1), 69-92.

Goldring, E. B., & Rallis, S. F. (1992, October). *Principals as environmental leaders.* Paper presented at the annual meeting of the University Council for Educational Administration, Minneapolis, MN.

Hallinger, P., Murphy, J., & Hausman, C. (1992). Restructuring schools: Principals' perceptions of fundamental educational reform. *Educational Administration Quarterly, 28*(3), 330-349.

Kirby, P. C., & Colbert, R. (1992, April). *Principals who empower teachers.* Paper presented at the annual meeting of the American Educational Research Association, San Francisco.

Lichtenstein, G., McLaughlin, M., & Knudsen, J. (1991). *Teacher Empowerment and Professional Knowledge.* New Brunswick, NJ: Consortium for Policy Research in Education.

Macpherson, R. J. S. (1989). Radical administrative reforms in New Zealand education: The implications of the Picot report for institutional managers. *Journal of Educational Administration, 27*(1), 29-44.

Manz, C. C., & Sims, H. P., Jr. (1984). Searching for the unleader: Organizational member views on leading self-managed groups. *Human Relations, 37*(5), 409-424.

Murphy, J. (1992). School effectiveness and school restructuring: Contributions to educational improvement. *School Effectiveness and School Improvement, 3*(2), 90-109.

Murphy, J. (1994). Transformational change and the evolving role of the principal: Early empirical evidence. In J. Murphy & K. S. Louis (Eds.), *Reshaping the principalship: Insights from transformational reform efforts* (pp. 20-53). Thousand Oaks, CA: Corwin.

Peterson, K., & Solsrud, C. (1993, April). *Leadership in restructuring schools: Six themes on the worklives of principals and teachers.* Paper presented at the annual meeting of the American Educational Research Association, Atlanta, GA.

Prestine, N. A. (1991a, April). *Completing the essential schools metaphor: Principal as enabler.* Paper presented at the annual meeting of the American Educational Research Association, Chicago.

Prestine, N. A. (1991b, October). *Shared decision making in restructuring essential schools: The role of the principal.* Paper presented at the annual conference of the University Council for Educational Administration, Baltimore, MD.

Rinehart, J. S., Short, P. M., & Johnson, P. E. (1994). *Empowerment and conflict at school-based and non-school-based sites.* Paper presented at the annual meeting of the American Educational Research Association, New Orleans, LA.

Schmuck, R. A., & Runkel, P. J. (1994). *The handbook of organization development in schools and colleges* (4th ed.). Prospect Heights, IL: Waveland.

Smylie, M. A. (1992). Teacher participation in school decision making: Assessing willingness to participate. *Educational Evaluation and Policy Analysis, 14*(1), 53-67.

Smylie, M. A., & Crowson, R. L. (1993). Principal assessment under restructured governance. *Peabody Journal of Education, 68*(2), 64-84.

Stanford, G., & Roark, A. E. (1974). *Human interaction in education.* Boston: Allyn & Bacon.

Terry, R. W. (1993). *Authentic leadership: Courage in action.* San Francisco: Jossey-Bass.

Weindling, D. (1992). Marathon running on a sand dune: The changing role of the head teacher in England and Wales. *Journal of Educational Administration, 30*(3), 63-76.

4

Opening Moves and Creative Structures

I had a little drawing of geometric figures—circles. I went to the faculty, put that picture up, and said, "This circle is the administration, this is the staff, this is the students, and these are the parents and community." I said, "What we want to do is to push the circles together so that we will share in decision making, so that I will no longer be at the top of a pyramid."

—Elementary school principal

We shy away from departmental representation on the leadership team. Instead, the people are elected at large by the entire faculty to represent the schoolwide faculty. You see, we didn't want to create a structure that was going to reinforce a traditional system that isn't designed for the 21st century. . . . There is so little effort at the high school level to share ideas and information across departments! We even send students out into the world with very fragmented understandings, with little grasp of ideas and concepts. Now, they [teachers] have a sense of loyalty to the liaison groups.

—High school principal

In Chapter 1, we discussed what shared governance means to principals; in Chapter 2, the factors that provide impetus to shared-governance initiatives; and in Chapter 3, the principal's new role. Yet the development of professional community in a school requires many structural changes, including changes in leadership to support the coordination of the espoused mission, encouragement of interdependence of teachers, deprivatization of practice, and empowerment for all teachers. In this chapter, we discuss fundamental structural changes that support shared-governance initiatives and thereby avoid the pitfalls of a hierarchical structure, which gives only a few teachers power—without checks and balances—and leaves others feeling powerless.

Becoming an innovative school "on the fly" is a challenge that some liken to "changing the tire on a moving bus" (Lonnquist & King, 1993). The most delicate aspect of this work, according to the principals we studied, is being able to *surrender power* at times when almost any *topic* of critical (or routine) concern is under consideration. This issue is discussed in the following section and precedes a discussion of issues related to the structure (and its elements) of shared-governance initiatives. We also describe highlights of the shared-governance structures found in our study schools, and finally, we discuss related structural issues and dilemmas faced by shared-governance principals and teachers.

Surrendering Power
Over a Variety of Issues

One Among Equals

During the early transition phases to shared governance, principals *learn* to back off—to give up *power* in order to become "one among equals"—and to take on a *supportive,* and ultimately freeing, role:

> Oh, I definitely have *less power* than I did before. Teachers are interested in what I have to say as an administrator with a global viewpoint, but ultimately, the majority of the power rests with the classroom teachers. People now defer to what they believe is best.

> One of the reasons I've been a student adviser, just like the teachers, this year is because the faculty still has difficulty listening to me as just an equal. It's that *position power.* But all I want to do is share, talk, just like everybody else. And I say, "Please don't listen to me as if I am 'the principal.'" We're still working through that.

> I've learned that our school has a very political environment, but it's a different kind of politics. We all have to communicate better

and be more cognizant of listening. It's a much more social process. And now, since decisions are made by the larger body, it *frees* me. If someone says, "Why did you do that?" I say, "Hey, we're all making this decision; remember me—I'm just *one* vote."

I think I have been a kind of *controller,* but now I try to not give a lot of my own input because I want decisions to be teacher initiated. Once, when I was assistant principal, I took the teacher-developed plan and rewrote it—and I felt really awful. But I have learned and grown. Shared governance has taken some of the *pressure* off of me, and it's so good. Now, for example, if they say, "What do you think?" I say, "No, what do *you* think?" Now teachers are not afraid to come to me and say, "This is what I think we should do." And our conflict is good conflict.

One thing we had to do the first year was to redefine the roles of the assistant principal, the department chairpersons, and me, the principal. We *are all part* of the shared-governance decision making, but our role is to carry out the decisions made.

Shared-governance principals realize the leadership potential of teachers and thus frequently *step out of the role of chair* or leader of the school's decision-making council to support teacher leadership:

The whole time the former principal was here she was the chairperson of the leadership council. Midyear of my first year as principal I said to the group, "I really think I shouldn't be running these meetings. I'm just *one of the group,* and you don't need to always look to me." It just looked like "the principal's committee," and I think they were afraid that if I voted one way and they didn't vote that way, that somehow it would be held against them. Now this year is the first that we've had a teacher leader, and it went really well. It's symbolic, and it helps teachers feel empowered.

Some principals found it advantageous to even *surrender* their liaison group membership:

The assistant principal is in a liaison group, but I'm not. The feeling was that the principal's presence *might stymie* the discussion. I used to be in a liaison group and not a lot of controversy ever came out of my group. I'm the one who proposed that maybe my presence stifled their [teachers'] willingness to express ideas on tough issues.

I'm not part of a liaison group and never have been. And often when the liaison groups are meeting and talking, I physically *leave the room.*

One principal acknowledged the role of key players among the faculty. While being careful to avoid favoritism, this principal often involved such people in early deliberations on important issues:

> I've got a whole section in my dissertation that I frequently stop and read to myself. It's about change. It's so important for administrators to understand that there are informal structures within the formal structures in a school. In shared governance, it plays out in knowing who the key players are, who has *informal power.* That person might have lots of rapport with the staff, has been here a long time, or for one reason or another has sway over others. And I'll say, "Why don't we run this by [that key player] and see what he or she thinks?" Sometimes it's fruitless, like lobbying Congress; it's difficult getting something going if the faculty isn't sold on the idea. I'm not talking about manipulating people or being hypocritical; it's more like tilling the ground, and staff members do the same kind of thing.

Topics of Concern: From Routine to Critical

In the shared-governance schools we studied, governing councils, liaison groups, and task forces deal with a *variety* of issues—scheduling, student achievement, discipline, personnel selection (including selection of administrators), teacher observations, and even budget:

> The first task force we had, believe it or not, actually *restructured the school day.* I didn't think their plan would work, and it's not perfect, but it's better than what we had. Back in the old days, the principal would have said, "This is how we're going to structure the day."

> The liaison groups met, and then the PSIT [Program for School Improvement Team] met. The PSIT works with instructional initiatives. At first, two things kept coming up: *test scores and student control.* Having students be silent in the halls wasn't my idea of what we should be focused on, but it took a couple of years to go from issues the former principal allowed them to discuss to more important issues. I had questioned asking a child to walk without talking—"but the teachers talk," I said. Well, that didn't go over too big. The next year we had a discipline task force that came up with a citizenship unit. That and student achievement were discussed in liaison groups, modified, then brought back to the PSIT and finally "voted" on, but it's really more of a consensus. By the time

an issue has gone through all of that, we've reached consensus on it. Rarely do we really vote.

The Committee for School Improvement deals with *almost any instructional issue* brought up. Oftentimes it comes to me from the central office, and if it's going to affect kids, I give it directly to the chairperson. I see myself as the implementer of [administrative] policy; they [teachers] don't want to do those things.

The Instructional Council developed a schoolwide *discipline program* to deal with student disrespect. Through our formal system of records, we realized it wasn't working, that something else needed to take place, because the same students were repeating bad behaviors. The group came up with the idea of an after-school program—media club, bookworms, step team, and chorus. We got faculty members to volunteer to do little after-school things to help deal with discipline problems.

We have *personnel* task forces. For instance, the art teacher became pregnant and left. So we asked the group, "Who would like to work on selecting a new art teacher?" Generally, we have quite a large group of people volunteering for that sort of thing.

The Team for School Improvement set up a *selection* committee for our two administrative leadership [assistant principal] vacancies. We sat around this table and interviewed 10 candidates. We had an honest, open discussion—the level of trust is pretty high here. The group even suggested new titles for them: assistant principal for classroom practice and assistant principal for organizational climate and culture.

Department chairpersons, assistant principals, and a couple other leadership people do 70% of our *teacher observations*. We haven't gotten very far down the road with that yet, but we believe that teacher behavior changes if we do observations as peer professionals. It's growth to become better teachers.

An Ideal Design for Democracy in Schools

The League of Professional Schools' hybrid democracy is based on both *representation* and *direct participation.* Elected and/or volunteer persons represent groups of teachers, counselors, support staff, parents, and community groups; together they deliberate and make decisions for all groups. In direct participation, people who wish to participate in a particular decision attend a designated meeting, decide on priorities and topics of study, and schedule meetings for large-group and all-school decision making.

We noted that most league schools aspire to (but some have not yet attained) a *hybrid form of democracy,* which includes a representative governing council (see Figure 4.1). This council identifies priorities, establishes task forces, and sets time lines. Final decisions require a referendum of the group as a whole.

The kind of council that usually serves by administrative appointment (such as one composed of department, team, or grade-level leaders) and that conducts administrative business—but that serves the interests of the various political domains—is *not* a democratic form of governance. Rather, a democratic council is

> a governing structure of freely elected or volunteer members who represent the school across grade levels, departments, and community lines, with the sole mission of figuring out the best education for all children, regardless of the current organizational, grade-level, and departmental lines. (Glickman, 1993, p. 42)

Under such circumstances, everyone can be involved, but *no one has to be involved* in decision making. However, all people *must comply* with decisions once they are made, and all people have the *right to try to change decisions* through democratic processes.

Glickman (1993) describes the "hybrid governance" design in this way:

> A *school council* is composed of elected members or volunteers (with the exception of the principal, who is an automatic member). The council establishes priorities and commissions *task forces* of volunteers (composed of faculty, students, parents, and others) to deliberate and make recommendations to the council. Once the task force makes its recommendation, its job is done. The council then studies the recommendation and asks each of its members to discuss the recommendation with *liaison groups,* for further input. Liaisons are all the members of the school community, organized into small groups, who serve as communication links to assigned council representatives. In this way, the council receives communication from the entire body about a recommendation. After such feedback, the school council, according to its decision-making rule, can either approve the recommendation or take it to the body at large for a final vote. (p. 41)

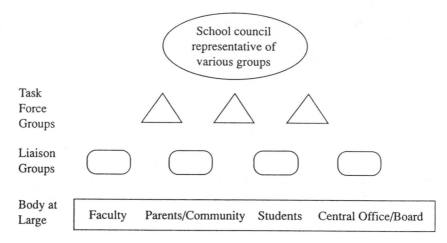

Figure 4.1. Hybrid Governance
SOURCE: From *Renewing America's Schools: A Guide for School-Based Action,* p. 41,
by C. D. Glickman, 1993, San Francisco: Jossey-Bass. Reprinted with permission.

The League of Professional Schools posits this set of governing
conditions for its ideal form of governance:

♦ One person, one vote

♦ No ultimate veto for any individual

♦ A decision-making rule to determine what is the necessary
vote to finalize a decision (e.g., majority, two thirds, consensus)

♦ Ratification of the process, structure, and decision-making
rule by the body at large (i.e., 80% vote "yes" by secret ballot
to initiate shared governance)

Characteristics of Effective
Shared-Governance Initiatives

In our book *Empowering Teachers: What Successful Principals
Do* (1994), we described characteristics of effective shared-governance initiatives. We noted that schools in the league attain these
characteristics to varying *degrees,* and they assign different *labels*

to the various characteristics. The design reproduced in Figure 4.2 is for your reference; it can also be compared with the school governance structures described by the principals we studied.

Governing Council
Structures in Study Schools

The formal governance structures adopted by the schools we studied varied somewhat, but all were generally designed after the hybrid governance structure set forth by the League of Professional Schools. The Oglethorpe County (Georgia) High School hybrid model, which features an executive committee and liaison groups, is a long-standing exemplar of shared governance and is emulated by many league schools. Highlights of the governance structures of our study schools are summarized here (names of schools are pseudonyms).

Cedar Creek High School. This school changed the name of its governing group from the Executive Council (thought to sound "elitist") to the *Team for School Improvement (TSI)*. The TSI consists of the principal, eight elected faculty and staff members (the pool for this council includes the school's dietitian and a secretary who beat three teachers in an election), and two parents and two students elected by the parent/student organization. Liaison groups are formed by cross-sectional groups of faculty and staff, the Parent, Teacher, Student Association (PTSA), and the student government. The principal is *not* a member of a liaison group but serves as liaison to the central office and the school board. Decisions are reached by consensus, if possible. (See Figure 4.3 for an excerpt from Cedar Creek High School's Statement of Purpose and Objectives for the TSI.)

Hagerty High School. The *Instructional Leadership Team* at Hagerty High School consists of the principal and nine representatives (each elected from liaison groups that include faculty, staff, counselors, and media personnel but no parents or students). Task forces are formed by volunteers or are recruited by team members who think that certain individuals' talents are suited to dealing with a particular issue.

Impetus

A faculty/staff/parent/student council is formed under the leadership and support of the principal *or* by teachers with the principal's agreement. In rare cases, a district dictates a shared-governance initiative.

Membership

Members of the council are elected or, less frequently, appointed by the principal in the early months. Infrequently, council members are the department or grade-level chairpersons, or the chairpersons may serve *in concert* with the regular council members.

Representation

Members of the council represent the school community at large, and each member's liaison group is formed randomly, with faculty, staff, parents, and students participating. *Committee* membership is voluntary, allowing people to choose to participate on committees of interest.

Scope of Authority

Effective shared-governance principals extend advisory and/or decision-making rights to representatives and their groups, according to agreements. Clarification of areas of advice and decision making occurs early in a shared-governance initiative; however, the formality of such agreements varies among schools. Formal power is typically given by the principal rather than the board of education, although the board may formally sanction shared-governance or "site-based" councils. In advanced shared-governance settings, power is assumed to be shared by all, thus equalizing the authority of administrators and teachers, and group decisions are implemented regardless of the principals' personal disposition.

Chairperson

Council members elect a chairperson, who is seldom the principal, except during the early stages of the shared-governance initiative.

Principal's Role

The principal is usually a member of the council but is "one among the many" and holds only one vote on issues discussed.

Figure 4.2. Characteristics of Effective Shared-Governance Initiatives

SOURCE: From *Empowering Teachers: What Successful Principals Do,* pp. 41-43, by J. Blase and J. R. Blase, 1994, Thousand Oaks, CA: Corwin Press. Reprinted with permission.

Meetings

Regular (at least quarterly) meetings are held at times convenient for the council members (in some cases consideration for release time is given, as for the annual in-depth planning session of the council). Agendas are distributed to all school personnel, invitations are issued, and regular communications, including minutes of the meetings, are distributed. These meetings are characterized by openness to new ideas, a nonthreatening atmosphere, and problem solving that uses action research.

Goals

The mission of the shared-governance council centers on *instructional improvement,* although significant time may be devoted to structural and administrative matters of concern during the early stages of the initiative. Annual discussion of the goals of the school and regular discussions of matters of import to all school community members take precedence over all other matters.

Staff Development

A significant element in successful shared-governance initiatives is the presence of major staff development programs. Staff development includes sessions on communication, group development skills, problem solving, decision making, and teacher leadership. During the beginning phases of the initiative, council members may derive such information from other schools or consortia with similar initiatives; less frequently this information is derived from districtwide staff development programs. Teachers usually take an active role in defining and implementing staff development.

Matters of Consideration

In well-developed shared-governance initiatives, the focus of the council's deliberations extends beyond technical and managerial matters to schoolwide improvement and instructional matters. In these advanced decision-making situations, critical issues, such as instructional budgeting and hiring of faculty and staff, are included in the responsibilities of council members.

Figure 4.2. Continued

Bullock Middle School. This middle school formed its *Committee for School Improvement* in an at-large election among volunteer teachers. The six resulting members also lead cross-disciplinary, cross-grade liaison groups that focus entirely on instructional matters. The chair of the committee is elected by the faculty, and the principal is a member.

Mitchell Middle School. Similar to Bullock Middle School's committee, the Mitchell Middle School *Executive Committee* consists of the principal and five elected chairpersons from the school's cross-sectional, randomly formed liaison groups. One administrator belongs to each liaison group.

Leathers Middle School. This school has a 13-member *Leadership Council,* which is considered the school's "umbrella" decision-making group, although there is also an Instructional Improvement Council. The Leadership Council consists of 6 liaison group leaders (each representing 15-20 faculty and staff members), 5 chairpersons of grade levels/special classes/exploratory classes, the chair of the Instructional Improvement Council, and the principal. The council includes any personnel volunteering to serve.

Casey Middle School. Casey's *Faculty Leadership Committee,* which prides itself on its history of consensus building (having resorted to voting only three times in 4 years), is composed of several teaching teams and exploratory area representatives, two parents (with only one vote), two students (elected, with only one vote), and two administrators (including the principal; they have two votes). This group of 20 listens to "briefs" and "rationales" regarding curricular, program, and financial matters; reviews priorities; and gathers feedback from the faculty and staff at large on such matters. In what they consider an administrator-proof process, ideological, philosophical, and pragmatic aspects of issues are explored, those without political lobbies (i.e., persons with special assignments, such as the school psychologist) are supported, and the trust level is high.

Bonner Elementary School. Bonner Elementary School's Program for School Improvement Team (PSIT) replicates the league's model, with a seven-member Executive Council (including the principal), seven liaison groups, and ad hoc task forces. The PSIT focuses solely on schoolwide instructional issues. A separate Leadership Team deals with "administrivia" or grade-level issues. A special *Advisory Committee* composed of the principal, two teachers, one classified representative, one business community representative, one community member who has no children, and six parents confer about schoolwide issues. A unique aspect of this Advisory Committee is the deliberate placement of parents *in numbers equal to the other members* on the committee.

Acorn Elementary School. Although parents are invited to attend meetings of Acorn Elementary's *Instructional Council, they cannot vote on decisions. The council consists of the principal, an elected faculty chairperson, one secretary, grade-level representatives, one specialist, and one Chapter 1 program representative. Task forces are formed as needed to address major instructional concerns, and cross-level study groups collect and analyze data to be used in discussions on topics of interest.*

Ridley Elementary School. This school has a comprehensive Building Level Team consisting of the principal, four faculty members (teachers from both multiage and traditional classrooms), one counselor, one specialist, one classified/custodian representative, one parent, and one student. Task forces are commissioned and dissolved as needed.

Most elected and appointed governing council members in the schools serve for two or three years, with some members rotating off the council each year to ensure continuity.

Structural Issues and Dilemmas

Such issues as membership on various councils and committees, voting, and potentially explosive topics were discussed by the principals we studied.

Membership Issues

The *central governing council* in shared-governance schools may originate in a variety of ways, including appointment, election, and self-nomination:

When we first began shared governance, I felt it was important to have a group of unquestionably committed people on the Leader-

CEDAR CREEK HIGH SCHOOL
School Improvement: Organization, Responsibilities,
and Procedures

Introduction
The faculty has voted to become a member of the League of Professional Schools and to adopt shared governance as the preferred method of governing the school in the future. A long-term school improvement plan is now to be implemented. The plan is premised on shared decision making and total staff and administration involvement for improving learning opportunities for all Cedar Creek High School students.

We believe that the following plan is an exciting and valuable one that will benefit all of us, particularly the students of our school.

Statement of Purpose
The Purpose of the Team for School Improvement is

1. to provide for shared decision-making between staff, parents, and administration relating to schoolwide improvements,
2. to provide for a free flow of communication between and among staff, parents, and administration, and
3. to provide for improved learning opportunities for students.

Objectives

1. to provide an ongoing means for initiating and supporting schoolwide improvement;
2. to provide systematic opportunities for staff, parents, and administration to develop consensus;
3. to move toward consensus among staff, parents, and administration;
4. to promote a sense of ownership or organizational goals among staff, parents, and administration;
5. to provide formal procedures for gathering valid information for problem identification, decision making, and problem-solving activities; and
6. to increase the level of harmony between individual and staff goals.

Figure 4.3. Purpose and Objectives of Cedar Creek High School Team for School Improvement

ship Team. *I appointed the people* who went to the statewide meeting to the team. The other half of the *team was elected,* and my appointees rotated off within three years. Still, the ones remaining were dubbed "the chosen few," and they became frustrated and were ready to quit because some of their colleagues couldn't get away from that terminology. So the teachers—just teachers—had a meeting to air all the dirty linen and hash the thing out. After that meeting the label went away, and now it's an artifact from the past. The meeting cleared the air.

The Leadership Team members are *self-nominated* and they campaign for office. The idea behind that was to be sure it's not a popularity contest. If you nominate yourself, you're more committed. We felt pretty good about that, but currently, we don't have a lot of people nominating themselves. We also have four nominees for only three positions, and it may be awkward for the one person to lose. It's evolutionary, though. We're struggling right now, but just like Russia can't get it all done in 5 years, we need time.

The biggest issue was about how many representatives to the *Building Level Team* came from multiage-classroom teachers and how many came from traditional-classroom teachers. They are competing for power in the school. It took a couple of months of fighting back and forth and beating each other over the head mercilessly until we finally *reached consensus* on something we could all live with.

By *consensus,* it was decided that assistant principals are not on the *Leadership Council.* They're not allowed to go to the meetings anymore. They got kicked off because the members said we had too many administrators talking on the council.

Generally, in schools that are members of the League of Professional Schools, cross-sectional *liaison groups* are standing, but *task forces* are formed, complete their work, and are disbanded according to need. Likewise, we found this true of the schools that we studied.

We're still a traditional high school in a lot of ways. People spend most of the day within their departments. But we've broken down some barriers by mixing it up in our *liaison groups.* People from different walks, different jobs or departments, come together. It happens on *task forces,* too. A math person, a vocational person, and a secretary sit down together.

We don't have a bunch of committees standing around collecting dust. Volunteers for *task forces* are solicited by an Instructional Leadership Team member. Anyone can be on any task force that interests them. It's a work group, a problem-solving group. They go out and do their homework, and then they bring the information to the ILT. If no more work is needed, it goes out to the *liaison groups* just to see how people feel. Or it might go directly to the faculty for a vote. If the faculty passes it, it's implemented, and the task force goes out of existence.

The only *task force* that remains in effect is our 5-year improvement plan task force. The plan is pretty complicated, and even though the whole faculty accepted it, we wanted to be sure there would be somebody around consistently to make sure we move along and accomplish our goals.

Membership on task forces is variously encouraged, debated, or dictated across the league schools we studied. Sometimes specific teachers are actively solicited as members, as illustrated in the following principal's comment:

Faculty members will go out and informally encourage certain people to be members of *task forces*. We have one guy with strong organizational skills who didn't step forward, but the others knew how good he was and wanted his skills for the six-period-day task force. He got invited by his fellow teachers to be on the task force, and he ate it up.

To Vote or Not to Vote

As noted earlier, people in shared-governance schools try to avoid voting on issues; instead, they seek a consensus in making decisions:

The Leadership Council doesn't really vote a whole lot. A lot of our decisions are reached by *consensus*; we just *talk* about it until we're all happy with it. We have a very vocal faculty, and they really share a lot. Now, sometimes the consensus will be to take the issue back to the liaison groups for their recommendation. We decide on a *case-by-case* basis.

We prefer *not voting* on issues because then there tend to be *winners and losers.* We prefer trying to reach *consensus.* You know, Can we all agree on this? Is there anything you absolutely cannot live with? If so, can we work on a way to change it?

In some schools, the democratic approach is reflected in representative voting:

There are about five high schools in the nation that have attempted to use the federal government as a model for the way they run the school, but they are not yet truly democratically based like we are. Here we vote and actually have *people represent people*. We're going to try to get a real representative body of the students here next fall; kids are going to feel empowered.

The liaison groups' purposes include communication and decision making. When we do *vote* on things as a whole faculty, it's done most of the time *in liaison groups*—but not always. Sometimes the voting is done by secret ballot. There's nothing in the constitution that says which way it has to be done.

One principal shared an example of an occasion when neither consensus nor voting occurred:

There are times when you can't wait two or three weeks for the Committee for School Improvement to make a decision. I was on the phone with a central-office person who needed somebody for the calendar committee immediately. *So I told the assistant principal that the next person to walk in the office would be it.* That's what happened, and we had a big laugh about it. We have that kind of relationship, though; I can't think of a person I would ask to do something who would say no.

Touchy Topics

Although ideas generally percolate up to the school council through liaison groups, some schools that we studied also use suggestion boxes and informal channels through the principal to *unearth concerns* that may be sensitive:

My door is usually open, and it's like Baskin-Robbins, seven or eight teachers lined up all the time. They just want to *talk* and not go through a formal channel. Then I might go to the Instructional Improvement Committee and say, "I've kind of heard. . . ." If something is bothering someone and he or she doesn't want to wait for the monthly liaison group meeting, they come to *me*.

We have a *suggestion box* system that we implemented this year. A task force lists the suggestions; the council votes on the month's best suggestion. It is implemented, and the person who suggested it gets a $25 gift certificate.

How do ideas come up to the council? A lot of times somebody *just says*, "Gee, whiz, the cafeteria is really getting awful." Or somebody might put a note in the *"buzz box,"* which is opened at PSIT meetings. Then it may be an issue for discussion, or it may come to me. But we respond to it, and people know something happened.

Members of the League of Professional Schools also dedicate considerable time to studying their schools—even if it hurts—and relevant professional literature and research reports to deal with sensitive topics:

> We're doing research, trying to find out what's going on. For example, I noticed the chalkboards in many classes full of [assignments for] seat work first thing every morning, and wondered if that's causing some of our disruptions. The task force members went through the building twice, taking a quick run through to see what people were doing for the morning. It created a little bit of conflict, but after a little explaining, everyone understands. We're looking at a learning process, and we're *collecting data* by committee regarding disciplinary matters also. At first teachers were angry, really upset, at the paperwork and recording of data. But then they realized that these are some real things that are going on, and they started talking about strategies to use to help. We realized we needed to look at the cause of problems rather than the symptoms.

> We have an *action research task force*. It studies to see if we are really making a difference. They produce a "school report card," and they demonstrate that kids are achieving, so we get "pay for performance" money from the state. We know we need to use lots of indicators to measure our success, so the task force is a permanent group now.

> What we have said in our meetings is that if we are truly going to be professionals, we need to do more *research*. We copy articles, get in our little huddles, and like a jigsaw, bring it all together in the whole group. We say what we've learned . . . we're actually *studying together.*

Ironies

Interestingly, when people in a school become empowered, some seemingly incongruous events may occur. For instance, shared governance often brings deeper discussion (hence more conflict), improved performance (hence more envy and criticism from the outside), and a challenge to maintain peak performance (hence more work). Glickman (1990) has documented seven ironies associated with empowered schools:

1. The more an empowered school *improves,* the more apparent it is that *there's more* to be improved.
2. The more an empowered school is *recognized* for its success, the more nonempowered schools *criticize* it.
3. The more an empowered school works *collectively,* the more individual differences and *tensions* among the staff members become obvious.
4. The more an empowered school becomes a *model* of success, the *less* the school becomes a practical model to be *imitated* by other schools.
5. The more a school becomes *empowered,* the more it *hesitates* to act.
6. The more an empowered school has to *gain,* the more it has to *lose.*
7. The more an empowered school resembles a *democracy,* the more it must *justify* its own existence to the most vocal proponents of democracy.

Comments of the principals in our study reflected many of these ironies. These principals also addressed several troubling states in their school's efforts to share governance. In their words,

Enthusiasm brings overload.
  We had something like 40 committees—subject area, calendar, technology, volunteers, staff development, action research, multicultural, wellness, publications, special events committees. We had so many committees we didn't know what to do. What we discovered about shared governance is that when everybody is making all these decisions and on all three different committees, it's tremendously time-consuming. So we *consolidated committees,* and we *consolidated meeting schedules.* Now we hold one Leadership Team meeting and one faculty meeting a month; it's very tight, and representatives who want to get an agenda item in do it early. Actually, it was a staff member who said, "These committees can be collapsed so we're not all running crazy."

Talk brings conflict.
  Five years ago there wasn't the great deal of discussion of issues that we now have. There is a lot of information exchange. When

you open up the decision making for participation, people need to get informed about the intricacies and fine details of issues, like a senator or congressman [sic] does to get ready to vote on an issue in our Congress. It's the same thing at the school level. Of course, when you start discussing tough issues, conflicts arise. Some people are afraid of conflict; they'd rather shove it back down. But it's good in another sense because things get out and are talked about.

Discussions on planning bring critique.

Some people make the assumption that if a discussion takes place, there's going to be immediate action on that issue. If an action doesn't come about, some people say, "Oops, too many irons in the fire." But we're not really doing those things. Sometimes we're just getting information, and we move things from the front burner to the back burner. Congress has a thousand deals in the hopper, but it's not going to pass all those bills at one time or even this year. Sometimes we move very fast, but other times, the process is slow because we don't want to make mistakes or fail to bring everybody along with us.

Polishing up an imperfect idea may create political backlash.

We've never had the Leadership Team make a wholesale rejection of a task force's recommendation, but they've said, "More work needs to be done; you've got some loose ends to tie up." That may not be politically wise, though, because the task force members are members of liaison groups and could cause a groundswell of support through the liaison groups, thus making for friction between the liaison groups and their chairs, who sit on the Leadership Team.

Barriers to Shared Governance: Cautions From Research

Though shared-governance approaches have at times led to improvements in the work climate, staff morale, and job satisfaction in schools (Evans & Perry, 1991), traditional patterns of power there have often remained *unchanged.* Shared-governance initiatives have been undermined in some schools by conservative *norms* of propriety and civility; ambiguous *role orientations* of principals, teachers, and parents on leadership councils; and the failure of efforts to seriously *involve* teachers and parents in decision making (Malen & Ogawa, 1988).

In case studies of schools in four districts, Robertson and Briggs (1994) also found three broad categories of problems that impeded effective decision making based on widespread involvement of staff: (a) *autocratic* tendencies on the part of the principal, who may have thought he or she was participative but who was, in fact, blocking authentic involvement; (b) existence of distinct *factions* with competing interests at the school (some who promoted reform, others who resisted it); and (c) *apathy* on the part of participants, notably staff members who did not wish to put energy into improving themselves or the school (see also Foster, 1991, about teacher reluctance to change).

Brown (1994) identified several additional barriers to shared governance, including fear of change among teachers and administrators, a lack of trust among teachers and between teachers and administrators, confusion concerning the roles that teachers and administrators should play, overbearing control by central-office administration, concerns about hidden agendas of central-office administration, and lack of support for teachers.

Clearly, innovative school organization and structure may promote teacher participation in decision making, but it does not guarantee teachers a meaningful role in such decision making. Among other things, resentful principals may hesitate to give decision-making bodies (particularly permanent groups, such as school site councils) decision-making power or even advisory power. And of course, giving decision-making discretion to a "select" group of teachers can become merely another form of administrative *control*. By creating the illusion of teacher decision making, control may become invisible. "Collaborative decision making" may become a new form of *domination* that is more insidious than that found in traditionally run schools (Flinspach, Easton, Ryan, O'Connor, & Storey, 1994; Hannaway, 1993).

Duke, Showers, and Imber (1980) found that teachers often feel that they have no real influence in decision making; rather they feel they are participating in the *illusion* of influence. Paradoxically, in some cases, other facilitative modes of decision making, such as ad hoc committees and informal participation (e.g., a chat with the principal), may yield real teacher participation. Imber and Duke (1984) suggest that traditionally organized schools with democratic principals may be among the better settings for conducing teachers' involvement and influence in decision making!

Furthermore, in a study of alternative models for involving teachers in decision making, Hallinger and Richardson (1988) reported substantial differences in the degree of empowerment existing under varying school governance structures. Structures in which teachers were vested with formally delegated authority (i.e., the Lead Teacher Committee and the School Improvement Team) provided significant access to power. The Instructional Support team model held significant potential for increasing teachers' instructional leadership but significantly limited their formal authority. By comparison, the Principal's Advisory Council structure, because of its noninstructional focus and reliance on the principal to delegate authority, provided no formal decisional authority to teachers.

In a large-scale study of site-based management, Malen and Ogawa (1988) found that school councils typically operated more as *advisory* groups and *pro forma endorsers* of principals rather than as decision-making bodies with authority. This research cited the principal's "controlling" leadership and teachers' obsequious orientation (often because of their fear of professional or social sanctions by the principal) as major barriers to shared governance.

Another major barrier to shared governance is lack of time. Shared governance requires sufficient time for collaborative decision making, that is, time to consult with all participants and time to fulfill one's responsibilities as principal, as one who has the responsibility for the school. The principals we interviewed reported that finding sufficient time for shared decision making is an ongoing challenge, but that wide involvement in decision making usually contributes to school improvement. These principals also reported having 60-hour work weeks, on average, a finding consistent with Hess's (1995) research.

Changing the Tire on a Moving Bus

As we have seen in this chapter, initiating democratic procedures and building structures to support shared-governance initiatives is incredibly challenging—akin to changing the tire on a moving bus! Before embarking on such a journey, principals, in concert with teacher leaders and parents, should consider these questions, the answers to which will ease the transition to shared decision making:

1. *Why engage* in shared decision making?
2. What *contextual* factors might complicate this effort?
3. What *barriers* to shared governance exist?
4. What is the view of the *central office* on shared governance?

5. How will teacher *autonomy* be enhanced?
6. How will teachers respond to greater *opportunities* to *participate in decision making*?
7. What *decision areas* will teachers engage in?
8. What will be the *scope of authority, involvement, and influence* of administrators, teachers, support staff members, parents, and community members?
9. How will students' personal and academic *lives be enhanced*?

References

Blase, J., & Blase, J. R. (1994). *Empowering teachers: What successful principals do.* Thousand Oaks, CA: Corwin.

Brown, D. F. (1994, April). *Experiencing shared leadership: Teachers' reflections.* Paper presented at the annual meeting of the American Educational Research Association, New Orleans, LA.

Duke, D., Showers, B. K., & Imber, M. (1980). Teachers and shared decision making: The costs and benefits of involvement. *Educational Administration Quarterly, 16*(1), 93-106.

Evans, W. J., & Perry, C. Y. (1991, April). *The impact of school-based management on school environment.* Paper presented at the annual meeting of the American Educational Research Association, Chicago.

Flinspach, S. L., Easton, J. Q., Ryan, S., O'Connor, C., & Storey, S. L. (1994, April). *Local school councils during four years of school reform.* Paper presented at the annual meeting of the American Educational Research Association, New Orleans, LA.

Foster, A. G. (1991). When teachers initiate restructuring. *Educational Leadership, 48*(8), 27-31.

Glickman, C. D. (1990). Pushing school reform to a new edge: The seven ironies of empowerment. *Phi Delta Kappan, 72*(1), 68-75.

Glickman, C. D. (1993). *Renewing America's schools: A guide for school-based action.* San Francisco: Jossey-Bass.

Hallinger, P., & Richardson, D. (1988). Models of shared leadership: Evolving structures and relationships. *Urban Review, 40*(4), 229-244.

Hannaway, J. (1993). Decentralization in two school districts: Challenging the standard paradigm. In J. Hannaway & M. Carnoy (Eds.), *Decentralization and school improvement: Can we fulfill the promise?* (pp. 135-162). San Francisco: Jossey-Bass.

Hess, A. G., Jr. (1995, April). *School management after five years in Chicago: The partnership of parents, community, and education.* Paper presented at the annual meeting of the American Educational Research Association, San Francisco.

Imber, M., & Duke, D. L. (1984). Teacher participation in school decision making: A framework for research. *Journal of Educational Administration, 22*(1), 24-34.

Lonnquist, M. P., & King, J. A. (1993, April). *Changing the tire on a moving bus: Barriers to the development of professional community in a new teacher-led school.* Paper presented at the annual meeting of the American Educational Research Association, Atlanta, GA.

Malen, B., & Ogawa, R. (1988). Professional-patron influence on site-based governance councils: A confounding case study. *Educational Evaluation and Policy Analysis, 10*(4), 251-270.

Robertson, P. J., & Briggs, K. L. (1994, April). *Managing change through school-based management.* Paper presented at the annual meeting of the American Educational Research Association, New Orleans, LA.

5

Expanding the Circle

Involving Others in Shared-Governance Initiatives

If we're going to have a democratic society, why not begin in our schools by modeling and involving people in democracy?
—High school principal

In order for parents to have high degrees of efficacy, schools must engage parents in the governance structure and go beyond the traditional role of "parent as audience."
—Madsen (1994, p. 9)

Principals, as "boundary spanners," must link the very permeable boundaries of the school with its environment. Today's reform movement places the school organization and its community in close contact, and principals spend more time interacting with parents, students, and community members (McPherson & Crowson, 1992). Goldring and Rallis (1993) identify three factors that support parental involvement in school governance:

1. The theoretical and practical assertion that educational organizations are *interconnected* with their environments
2. Research that demonstrates that parent participation is an *important component* of the "effective school"

3. Expanding literature on the relative *superiority* of schools with high parent involvement (e.g., private schools)

More than ever before, school principals are facing "a massive increase" in work with governing councils that include parents (Earley, Baker, & Weindling, 1990). Student involvement, on the other hand, is more rare. This chapter examines both parental and student involvement.

Empowerment for Parents

The principals we studied defined "empowered parents" as those who collaborated with educators to make decisions about their children's education. In traditional schools, however, parental involvement usually does not include decision making; common roles for parents are as teachers of their own children, classroom volunteers, paid professionals, learners (e.g., child-rearing skills), and audience (e.g., at assemblies and conferences) (Rhine, 1981).

Parents and teachers have different perspectives on parental involvement. Teachers often doubt that parents want to be substantially involved in schools. Although some parents who participate in schools in traditional ways (e.g., on advisory committees and through parent organizations) feel a high degree of efficacy (Greenwood & Hickman, 1991), parents often feel that schools should do more to involve them in significant ways (Epstein, 1986). Indeed, parents may feel extraneous, inferior, or even in awe of professional educators during decision-making meetings. Lieberman (1989) has recognized the tension that exists between parents and teachers, and the fact that parents have been "separated" for so long from the school by the educational bureaucracy. Nevertheless, she thinks that if teachers work with parents—respond to their input, especially— both groups can develop the capacity for greater "collective" confidence and knowledge.

Indeed, research has demonstrated that *active* parental involvement and influence in schools has the potential to promote significant social and academic change in schools (Comer, 1984). Effective restructuring efforts often emphasize parental influence in decision making through authentic participation, cooperation, and partnerships (Epstein, 1989).

Zimmerman and Rappaport (1988) have described empowerment as "a process by which individuals gain mastery or control over their own lives and democratic participation in the life of their community" (p. 726). Although parental *involvement* in shared governance is an important step toward empowerment, it may not lead to real parental *influence*. For example, serving on a school council by invitation rather than being elected to it affects a member's influence. An invitation to participate may provoke feelings of indebtedness in parents, possibly leading to reluctance to question the professional educators about school matters. Coupled with a lack of knowledge about school procedures and confusion about the limits of their power, parents may be reluctant to express themselves openly (Malen & Ogawa, 1988).

Goldring (1995) has described the levels of parental empowerment on a continuum ranging from passive to active, with access to information and selecting a school for their children as examples of passive parental empowerment. More empowered parents are involved in school activities, and the most empowered parents have substantial influence in decision making at the school.

Empowerment has been discussed by Goldring (1995) in terms of two dimensions: *relational* and *motivational*. In the latter, power resides within parents who want to effect changes in school decisions and develop meaningful partnerships with educators and others for change. Parents may provide guidance and resources to schools that value such assistance. In this sense, parent empowerment has been linked with satisfaction, involvement, and expectations (Goldring & Bauch, 1993). Conger and Kanungo (1988) have defined this dimension of empowerment as "a process of enhancing feelings of self-efficacy among organizational members through the identification [and removal] of conditions that foster powerlessness" (p. 474). In the *relational* view, empowerment is acquired when parents access the school's power base. Becoming a legitimate member of a school governance council is an example of this form of power.

Clearly, we are challenged as educators to accord parents more than ritualistic involvement in school life (e.g., after-school activities and open-house nights; see Swap, 1993). We must expand parental involvement beyond concerns with their own children and beyond "fund raising and social events that do not involve them in the core educational activities of the school" (Munn, 1993, p. 1). We must go beyond parental input to parental *influence;* this is true empowerment.

Starting Out

The initial decision to involve parents and students in the work of school councils, liaison groups, and task forces in the shared-governance schools we studied was somewhat problematic for educators. Principals in our study described the beginning discussions about parent and student involvement in their schools in a variety of ways. In some cases, these discussions were quite heated:

> We've had some knock-down, drag-out *fights* over the years about whether the Leadership Team should have parents and students or other staff members who may want involvement on it. Up until last year, the answer was an absolute, emphatic *"No."* [Teachers think,] "Nobody else is going to be a part of this." The idea was always rejected by the Leadership Team and also by the faculty when it was discussed in liaison groups. I was disappointed. The teachers have unfounded fears. I don't think parents want to run the school; they would like to have input, they would be honored to be involved, and they would make a better school.

> How do we teach kids to function in a democracy without allowing them to be *participants* in the democracy? Well, teachers argued, *"We can't have parents and students present;* they'll hear things they don't need to hear." Like what? I thought. We don't talk about individuals. Why can't we talk about things in front of and with these people? Last spring we did put parents and students on the task forces. They *study problems* and collect and *analyze data.* It's very powerful, and yet they're *still not on the Leadership Team.*

Sometimes parental involvement is limited because of the parents' traditional expectations of the principal:

> We have *no formal structures* that involve parents and students yet. We have involved parents in our Success Bound program; we brought them in for input, to share their ideas. But still, our parents' role is very *limited.* Once we get to the point that they understand how we govern ourselves—right now, they still think the principal is the lightning rod for everything—then they would be able to work with the Committee for School Improvement.

In other cases, parent and student involvement is viewed as less problematic:

Parents and students are *members* of our task forces. They reach consensus informally. The process is slow, and it sometimes becomes frustrating, but we don't want to go so fast that we make mistakes. We want to bring everybody along with us.

Parents and students *serve on our Team for School Improvement.* They also serve on most *task forces.* The students, in particular, were on task forces for discipline and appeals. That group gave teachers authority to suspend students; that forces teachers and students to deal with their problems instead of coming to an administrator. . . . And the appeals committee prevents teachers and students from getting into power struggles.

Our research indicates that even after several years of involvement in shared governance, principals who are eager to include parents in school decision making continue to confront barriers to authentic involvement, such as teacher reluctance, parent apathy, and student resistance:

You see, sometimes as educators we think the schools belong to us, when in fact they don't. They belong to the community. I'm disappointed that we have not empowered parents, that *we don't want the community to participate* in the institution that belongs to them.

The *teachers are a little bit reluctant* to put parents (and students) on the Leadership Council. They wouldn't be as open and honest with them there, and they wouldn't want parents to think that their haggling is animosity. It's not, but we get heated in our talks because people feel strongly about things.

Presently, we have one parent on the Leadership Council, and we've had difficulty getting other parents involved. The reason is *they don't really understand* the curriculum, and we're all talking about the particulars of the reading and writing program. A parent said, "As far as I'm concerned, you know what you're doing, you're teaching our children. Do I really need to sit through this whole meeting?"

Once the kids get to be middle school age, they begin to disassociate from their parents; *they don't want their parents hanging around the school.* But we've had parents doing fund raising and pizza parties, things like that. Then we tried more formal meetings combining the PTO and the Booster Club, trying to get a crowd here, but they'd leave after one part or the other. We now have a small group that is active, and they're helping with the bond issue, but you don't get a roomful of people.

I had parents in to help develop our philosophy and mission statement, but *we don't have a lot of parents come* into our school. Three parents volunteer in the media center, several come every morning to help with the breakfast program, and one bus driver comes to read to students (I put his talk about goals in our newsletter to parents), and Chapter 1 or Special Ed parents come in, but parents aren't involved in decision making in formal ways.

Some principals, however, have found that involving parents in school matters is easy:

In shared governance, the idea with parents is this: *You get them involved, and they learn to trust the school.* Then they will go anywhere with you, they will do anything, and they will trust you to do anything for them.

We involve parents in *lots of ways.* Teachers recommend parents, and parents who call with questions are invited to join the advisory committee. I also call the feeder schools and ask for recommendations. Our advisory now has all kinds of people on it—different socioeconomic levels, minorities, disabled students' parents. We get everybody involved.

One principal relied on the power of education to bring crucial parental involvement to school decision making:

We have to *educate* the parent clientele, so they see that their input is in the best interests of the school. *We need that input,* and we need it from a lot of different people.

Despite barriers to parental involvement, the principals we studied provided some evidence of *parental influence* in school decision-making processes:

We had *a lot of discussion* with parents about budget. Then we sent out a survey to see how parents felt about a project, and we had a 90% approval rate! We also got a long waiting list of parents to help us!

We have a very dynamic PTA, but the ISAC [Instructional School Advisory Council] was mandated by the superintendent, and the ISAC ended up having more power, on paper, than the PTA. With the dual structure, the members couldn't figure out what they wanted to do. I got permission to do away with the ISAC and then combine the two groups, but by then the ISAC had begun to function well. It's very powerful now; *when the ISAC speaks, the central office listens and the board listens* because it's the parents speaking. [ISAC requires that half its membership consist of parents.]

Last year's parent survey indicated that a lot of parents wanted more "skill and drill" in our interdisciplinary units. Now we call it "academic application," and teachers can include grammar or spelling lessons, for example. That was a *direct result of parent input.*

We have a voluntary school dress program whereby students wear uniforms. A group of *parents started the initiative,* and they contacted 90% of our parents. Ninety percent of them *wanted* uniforms! The parents went to the board, and they let us do it on a trial, voluntary basis for a year. We now have about 85% participation, and even teachers wear the school colors almost every day.

As a cautionary note, we point out that neither an "uncritical" appointment of parents to school decision-making teams by the principal nor the election of parents to a school council guarantees that equity issues (for example, issues that represent the *diversity* of the community) will be seriously addressed (Reitzug & Capper, 1993). However, without parental involvement in decision making, the probability of adequately addressing such issues is significantly reduced.

Degrees of Parental Involvement

Several large school systems (e.g., New York City, Chicago, Salt Lake City, St. Louis) recently established local school councils composed of parents and educators. Examining two of these reform experiments is helpful here because they illustrate very different degrees of parental involvement in school decision making.

The Chicago Experience: Parity Plus Power

Chicago's School Reform Act, adopted by the Illinois General Assembly in 1988, is based primarily on a theory of democratic control. As one current reform strategy, it represents "the devolution of authority from a large, centralized school district and its bureaucracy to a local, democratically elected governance unit at the school level" (Hess, 1995, p. 1). The Reform Act mandated that 14 school councils make up the governance structure of the district. Six members of the school governance council are parents, and the council chairperson is an elected parent. The Chicago councils also include two community representatives, and in the high schools, a student, the principal, and two teachers. Consequently, the parents and community members in the Chicago councils constitute the majority of the school council.

In the case of the Chicago schools, establishing a favorable environment for shared governance includes more than voting parity for parents and community representatives. It includes assigning councils governance responsibilities and the power needed to carry out those responsibilities. Therefore, the Chicago local school councils hire and evaluate principals, approve and monitor the school improvement plan, and budget the school's discretionary funds. Chicago school reform has converted parents and community representatives "from being 'advisors' with some power into being 'deciders' with ultimate authority on most issues" (Hess, 1991, p. 151).

From their research on Chicago school reform, Flinspach, Easton, Ryan, O'Connor, and Storey (1994) concluded that although "it is quite difficult to carry out site-based management so that lay constituents exert real decision-making authority, some Chicago councils have done so" (p. 22). Parents and community members on effective school councils in Chicago have displayed initiative by

- suggesting new ideas
- scrutinizing and questioning proposals
- offering to provide information
- carrying out committee work
- following through on council business
- helping execute council decisions
- helping to guide the council if needed
- attending council meetings regularly
- participating at length in discussions
- attending available training opportunities

After several years of studying site-based management in Chicago schools, Easton et al. (1993) described four types of council governance operating among the 14 representative councils.

Type 1: Limited Governance. This type of council governance is characterized by *unchallenged principal leadership,* minimal discussion of issues, and rubber-stamping of what school professionals have decided to do by parent and community leaders.

Type 2: Moderate Governance. Moderate governance is similar to Type 1 council governance: The principal dominates decision making, and the majority of parent and community representatives do not make suggestions about school improvement. However, Type 2 governance includes at least one parent or community member who *regularly exerts influence* on council decisions. Sometimes such an individual's efforts foster a more independent role for the council in decision making.

Type 3: Balanced Governance. In the balanced type of council governance, parents and community members and school professionals cooperate to *share influence* over decision making. The principal and chairperson share the leadership role, and most parents and community representatives are active participants.

Type 4: Excessive Governance. This type of council governance is associated with *unstable leadership* by parent and community members because of the weak status of the principal (due to interim status or lack of support). Council infighting about leadership and power issues is common, and clashes between factions divide the school community. Thus, decision making about significant issues is in constant dispute.

In our research, we found evidence of all four types of school governance described above. Approximations of balanced governance (Type 3) were most frequently apparent:

> We always *share with parents* what we're doing instructionally. We send out newsletters, progress reports, and special information about events like a writing contest.

> Our parents do not serve on the teachers' Leadership Council, but they do *serve on an active Parent Advisory Council* that makes decisions and has committees. For example, they developed our 10-page parent survey that asks parents to evaluate just about every program we have. We also have parents on our *Care Team,*

on our *Guidance Advisory Council,* and in *liaison groups* (which, by the way, also include custodians, cafeteria staff, et cetera).

Before, we had a few very vocal and very negative people who wanted to be in a position of power to make sure things were done their way. They always dominated. But when we started the liaison groups, they said, "Whoa! We appreciate your opinion, but we have one as well." Now they work for consensus from the groups. The power brokers have died out now, and *power is diffused.* And there's so much going on!

Parents and students are involved in our vision team. They sit on committees, are *fully involved* in the shared-governance process, and they give us important data back.

We frequently turn things over to *groups of parents* for decisions. They were *involved* in our mission statement and our goals; they helped us change them to fit our school exactly.

We have *a lot* of *informal* parent involvement. It's so much a part of our culture that almost everything we do has parent involvement. Like today, we're having teacher-of-the-year judging, and parents are here judging right along with teachers.

The *committee members* decide when they've reached consensus, and people trust the committees. When the goals, the action plan, and the assessment are all outlined, when *faculty and parents* all come to consensus on the issue, we're going to go with it.

Parents serve by giving input. They don't have a right to vote because there's not any voting that takes place! Right now we're working on a Home-School Partnership document, and parents are helping with that. They go out and get input from a random group of parents, and they will continue to gather input and talk about it until they get a document that people like and agree on.

I started the year by having a *parent forum* and just listening to what parents want. But I didn't want to have a PTA and another parent group, so now we just invite parents to come in to our Instructional Council meetings. The PTA is usually a show-and-tell kind of thing, but the IC [Instructional Council] is real shared governance.

Our parents serve on the *decision-making groups*—the task forces and committees. They give input on a *variety* of things. . . . In fact, every topic area except staff development had a parent involved.

According to some involved principals, the Chicago reform effort has produced internal politics they characterized as isolating and even "feudal," and they described the relationship with central-office personnel as increasingly remote (Crowson & Boyd, 1991). Apparently, to some principals, autonomy is experienced as isolation.

Lessons From Salt Lake City

In contrast to the general success of the Chicago schools' reform effort is the site-based governance in Salt Lake City schools reported in Malen and Ogawa's (1988) sobering case study. The study demonstrates that principals must go beyond establishing norms that support genuine openness. They must also *share* decisions and provide *training* in how to alter patterns of influence of teachers and parents. Despite support from central office, broad jurisdiction, and policy-making authority to deal with budgets, personnel, program evaluation, and other significant matters in the Salt Lake City schools, teachers and parents were not significantly influential in their role on school site councils. Malen and Ogawa (1988) cited three themes to explain the discrepancy between expected and discovered patterns of influence:

1. Although site councils were authorized policymakers, they functioned as *ancillary advisers* and pro forma endorsers. (Core and program issues received superficial attention; the focus was on supplemental activities; members merely listened or advised.)

2. Teachers and parents were granted parity in representation, but principals often *controlled* the partnerships. (Principals and educators directed agendas and merely shared information with parents; norms of propriety and civility maintained harmony but suppressed productive disagreement.)

3. When teachers and parents did have access to decision-making arenas, their inclusion *maintained*—but did not alter— the decision-making relationships found in traditional schools. (Council membership was rarely issue driven or change oriented; the principal maintained authority and was seldom challenged; and parent and chairpersons' involvement was clerical rather than substantive.)

Sadly, principals in Salt Lake City described the site councils as "channels for dispensing information, moderating criticisms, and garnering support, not as arenas for redefining roles, sharing power, and making policy" (Malen & Ogawa, 1988, p. 259).

Schools composed of economically and ethnically divergent populations often have school councils with only demographically and culturally similar members. This was the case in the Salt Lake City schools. The councils were, with rare exception, made up of Caucasian, middle-class, well-educated mothers; Caucasian teachers who had spent their careers in the district; and Caucasian principals who had previously served as teachers and counselors in the district (Malen & Ogawa, 1988).

Advice and Cautions

Findings from the Chicago and Salt Lake City schools are both advisory and cautionary with respect to establishing parent involvement in school decision making. We suggest the following:

1. *Listen carefully to the issues and concerns of parents.* A group of professional educators can easily intimidate a parent who has something to share. Modeling active listening skills is crucial to effective communication, and it demonstrates that parents are valued members of the educational team.

2. *Demonstrate respect for parents.* All parents have a contribution to make to the educational endeavor, and sincere mutual respect is the foundation for successful collaboration. Trust the expertise of parents, and use their input. Parental involvement and power should not be ambiguous or vaguely defined.

3. *Build a partnership.* Most schools are still organized as bureaucratic and hierarchical structures. Work to eliminate aspects of these models of organization that interfere with shared decision making in your school. Consider inviting parents to become members of your school's council as well as its advisory groups.

4. *Inform parents.* Parents cannot be expected to engage in meaningful discussions with educators without being given relevant information and data. Often the little information parents receive is obscured by educational jargon and technical terminology. Avoid distancing parents by keeping them ignorant of school programs.

5. *Share the vision.* Parents, administrators, teachers, and students should work together to build a commitment to their shared vision for the school. Ongoing discussions can renew that commitment and help to ensure that all vital interests are reflected in the vision.

6. *Welcome multiple views and conflict.* Parents should not be placed on the school's council as "token" representatives, nor should especially compliant or supportive parents always serve on the council. The interaction of people with diverse perspectives often brings the most progress. Strive to include strong parents on your council; they will encourage needed changes. Strive also to include parents from economically and ethnically divergent school populations.

7. *Be clear about agreements.* Ambiguity has no place in discussions among people representing many different perspectives. Become a model of specificity and clarity. As one of our study principals put it,

> Before I leave the table [when working with parents and others], I always "speak the agreement" before I go. I say, "From what I've heard, given our vision, this is our next goal and the direction we're going in, correct?" That way, before we leave the table, we are clear that we have agreed.

8. *Capitalize on the power of numbers.* Each person authentically involved in school decision making can inform and influence many others in positive ways on issues ranging from funding to instructional programs. One principal commented,

> Each school has a bond issue team. We found seven team teachers—parents and teachers—who each found five unit leaders. Then each unit leader found ten people who would vote positively for the bond issue. It worked like a pyramid. We've used the *same concept to gain support* for program proposals.

Student Involvement

Students are seldom included in school reform or shared-governance initiatives in meaningful ways. This merely compounds the effects of the current trend of diminishing student involvement in the schools. Davis and Ziegenhals (1995), for example, found that students decreasingly spend their free time in school-affiliated activities, such as clubs, spirit events, and co- and extracurricular activities. At the same time, diversity in student culture, race, ethnicity, family structure, and economic base makes it all the more necessary to involve students in determining needs and participating in decision making in schools. The principals in our study were struggling with the design and implementation of student governance structures:

> Students need *formal processes,* a student government council. The old one was an ineffective mechanism for change, and the kids didn't really know what they wanted. Now we have a new building and a new student body, and I'm looking forward to starting up a new group next year.

> Our governance structure has to include organizing *officers* and *representatives* from each grade. There's a *delicate balance to meetings*—meet periodically but not so much you run the kids off. Then it comes down to finding out what are their major concerns and what we can do to change and to enhance what's going on in our school.

> A lot of the things we talk about are of low interest to students, and they take a lot of time. Mostly we *operate separately unless a student issue comes up.* Then the student council comes forward, and the representatives do have a vote on the Instructional Team.

Clearly, student participation in school governance ranges from mere feedback to representation on school governing councils, but our data indicate that overall student influence in the schools we studied is relatively weak:

> We restructured the student government so that we have *representatives* from each class, but it's not really a governing board yet, *not* really an empowered group of folks yet. It's our weakest group, in terms of shared governance.

> I thought it would be a good idea to have a student serve on the Leadership Council, but *the teachers don't want students* at those meetings, even though they want student input. Our discussions in those meetings get pretty heated sometimes . . . people haggling it out. But at least our student council chairperson serves on the PTSA board, which is advisory to me.

> *No students* participate in our Instructional *Council,* but we have *bimonthly meetings* with select groups of students, like honor roll students.

Student input, when it does occur, ranges from functional concerns, such as furniture needs, to input on serious instructional matters:

> A sample of our student requests includes class meetings, better classroom discipline, doors on toilets, larger desks for chubby kids, recognition for teachers, a larger library, and repairs for playground equipment. We also get formal student input on items such as the Safe School grant, the media committee, and monthly surveys. Students especially liked the new gift shop, the book program, and the after-school program—all of which they recommended.

> We have *student representatives* from each of the galaxies [grade levels] who meet *regularly,* and we talk with them about a number of topics, like discipline, the cafeteria, and traffic flow. They bring up their concerns.

> Some teachers allow students to help them pick their thematic units, and some have students involved in a process of determining *class decisions* about what they'd like to know.

> Teachers do informal *curriculum assessments* or instructional *technique assessments* with them.

Interestingly, Gips and Wilkes (1995) found that teachers favor student involvement in site-based decision making but are unclear about what age or in what form such involvement should occur.

A Challenge

Changing the organizational and cultural structure of a school requires that participants be change agents who believe in the change, who feel they have an important part to play in its achievement, and who feel respected and valued by others. They must also embrace "the values, beliefs, norms, and habits of collaboration and continuous improvement" (Fullan, 1993, p. 131). The principals we studied (and those studied by others, e.g., Wohlstetter, Smyer, & Mohrman, 1994) are deeply involved in developing community understanding, acceptance, and pride in the changes under way. They also work hard to increase their school's visibility in the community. Such principals recognize their role in establishing trust, focusing on student needs, facilitating communication among all constituents, and conveying expectations and limitations. They understand the importance of developing a lasting commitment in others to reduce the possibility that, as one principal in our study remarked, "shared governance would be thought of as a passing fad."

References

Comer, J. P. (1984). Home-school relationships as they affect the academic success of children. *Education and Urban Society, 16*(3), 323-337.

Conger, J. A., & Kanungo, R. N. (1988). The empowerment process: Integrating theory and practice. *Academy of Management Review, 13* (3), 471-482.

Crowson, R. L., & Boyd, W. L. (1991). Urban schools as organizations: Political perspectives. In J. G. Cibulka, R. J. Reed, & K. K. Wong (Eds.), *The Politics of Urban Education in the United States* (pp. 87-103). London: Taylor & Francis.

Davis, D. E., & Ziegenhals, B. J. (1995, April). *Myth vs. reality: Identifying school needs in restructuring.* Paper presented at the annual meeting of the American Educational Research Association, San Francisco.

Earley, P., Baker, L., & Weindling, D. (1990). *"Keeping the raft afloat": Secondary headship five years on.* London: National Foundation for Educational Research in England and Wales.

Easton, J., Flinspach, S. L., O'Connor, C., Paul, M., Qualls, J., & Ryan, S. P. (1993). *Local school council governance: The third year of Chicago school reform.* Chicago: Chicago Panel on Public School Policy and Finance.

Epstein, J. L. (1986). Parent reactions to teacher practices of parent involvement. *Elementary School Journal, 86*(3), 277-293.

Epstein, J. L. (1989). *Effects of the teachers involving parents in schoolwork.* Baltimore: The John Hopkins University, Center for Research on Elementary and Middle Schools.

Flinspach, S. L., Easton, J. Q., Ryan, S. P., O'Connor, C., & Storey, S. L. (1994, April). *Local school councils during four years of school reform.* Paper presented at the annual meeting of the American Educational Research Association, New Orleans, LA.

Fullan, M. (1993). Innovation, reform and restructuring strategies. In G. Cawelti (Ed.), *Challenges and achievements of American education: 1993 Yearbook of the Association for Supervision and Curriculum Development* (pp. 116-133). Alexandria, VA: Association for Supervision and Curriculum Development.

Gips, C. J., & Wilkes, M. (1995, April). *Teacher concerns as they consider an organizational change to site-based decision making.* Paper presented at the annual meeting of the American Educational Research Association, San Francisco.

Goldring, E. B. (1995, April). *Empowering parents in schools.* Paper presented at the annual meeting of the American Educational Research Association, San Francisco.

Goldring, E. B., & Bauch, P. A. (1993, April). *Parent involvement and school responsiveness: Facilitating the home-school connection in schools of choice.* Paper presented at the annual meeting of the American Educational Research Association, Atlanta.

Goldring, E. B., & Rallis, S. F. (1993). *Principals of dynamic schools: Taking charge of change.* Newbury Park, CA: Corwin.

Greenwood, G. E., & Hickman, C. W. (1991). Research and practice in parent involvement: Implications for teacher education. *The Elementary School Journal, 91*(3), 279-288.

Hess, G. A., Jr. (1991). *School restructuring, Chicago style.* Newbury Park, CA: Corwin.

Hess, G. A. (1995). *School based management after five years in Chicago: The partnership of parents, community, and education.* Chicago: Chicago Panel on School Policy.

Lieberman, A. (1989). On teacher empowerment: A conversation with Ann Lieberman. *Educational Leadership, 46*(8), 23-26.

Madsen, J. (1994, April). *Parent efficacy in independent private schools: Lessons for public schools.* Paper presented at the annual meeting of the American Educational Research Association, New Orleans, LA.

Malen, B., & Ogawa, R. T. (1988). Professional-patron influence on site-based governance councils: A confounding case study. *Educational Evaluation and Policy Analysis, 10*(4), 251-270.

McPherson, R. B., & Crowson, R. L. (1992, November). *Creating schools that "work" under Chicago reform: The adaptations of building principals.* Paper presented at the annual meeting of the University Council for Educational Administration, Minneapolis, MN.

Munn, P. (1993). *Parents and schools.* London: Routledge.

Reitzug, U. C., & Capper, C. A. (1993, April). *Deconstructing site-based management: Possibilities for emancipation and alternative means of control.* Paper presented at the annual meeting of the American Educational Research Association, Atlanta, GA.

Rhine, W. R. (1981). *Making schools more effective: New directions follow through.* New York: Academic Press.

Swap, S. M. (1993). *Developing home-school partnerships: From concepts to practice.* New York: Teachers College Press.

Wohlstetter, P., Smyer, R., & Mohrman, S. A. (1994). New boundaries for school-based management: The high involvement model. *Educational Evaluation and Policy Analysis, 16*(3), 268-286.

Zimmerman, M. A., & Rappaport, J. (1988). Citizen participation, perceived control, and psychological empowerment. *American Journal of Community Psychology, 16*(5), 725-750.

6

The Driving Dream

Vision

School reform is determined by a confluence of several factors, including supportive district policy, viable collaboration between external and internal support structures, and "an initiating and strong principal who aids *vision-building* and creates procedures and structures which become structurally embedded [institutionalized]" (Miles & Ekholm, 1991, p. 10). The "driving dream," or vision, is essential, given the ambitious and complex nature of school reform: It articulates values, supplies direction, initiates activities, and provides standards for trouble-shooting problems that emerge in the hurly-burly work of implementing projects.

Shared leadership is considered essential to implementing vision. Brown (1994) learned that shared leadership was strongly related to

- *empowering faculty* and *sharing decision making;*
- developing a *shared mission,* identifying *common purposes,* establishing *common goals,* and developing *shared values;*
- ensuring more *open communication* and working *collaboratively;* and
- establishing clearly stated *roles* and sharing *expectations.*

In a study of the "courtship," or initial phase, of a systematic restructuring process (à la the accelerated schools model) in northwestern urban schools, Chenoweth and Kushman (1993) found that principals fulfilled their role of facilitating school vision by

- understanding the guiding principle of *unity of purpose* (personal visions became a *shared vision* of what purpose should be)
- becoming *promoters* and *keepers* of the *vision*
- *introducing* and *clarifying* the accelerated schools *model*
- creating a sense of urgency or a *press for school change* through involvement and modeling
- directing the vision at *teaching and learning*

Chenoweth and Kushman concluded that such actions by principals provided direction for the challenging and ambiguous restructuring efforts. Principals also prevented the means (that is, new governance structures) from becoming the ends of their work with others.

Without exception, the principals we studied agree that the development of a *shared vision* is critical to the success of a shared school governance:

> We all share the vision here. I even try to hire people inclined to a similar vision. They must believe in the process of empowerment, no ifs, ands, or buts. If they don't, they won't like it here.

A Critical Role

Conley's 1991 study of school restructuring and site-based decision making concludes:

> Principals in schools are serving as facilitators and developers, rather than bosses. They are involved in helping to create a *common vision* of the school, to model behaviors consistent with that vision, and to allocate resources and distribute information that helps the total school community move toward that vision. (p. 38)

Conley's research shows that vision emerges over varying lengths of time in different schools. At times, informal processes rapidly produce a mutually recognized statement of beliefs, feelings, and values. In one case, a principal created a three-word mission statement on his way to a school function, and faculty members endorsed it immediately because it reflected their collective beliefs. At other times, processes are quite slow; visions emerge only after as many as 3 years of work. Goldman, Dunlap, and Conley (1993) explain that vision building brings educators to mutual understanding, collective commitment, and consensus of direction. Silins (1994), who investigated relationships between leadership practices and school outcomes, found that transformational leaders affected teacher participation, productivity, commitment, and satisfaction because they were considered "visionaries." A leader is a visionary to the degree that she or he "creates a vision that elicits commitment and energizes people, perpetuates a common understanding of what the school is attempting to achieve for students, teachers, and parents, and is seen as having the ability to ensure they succeed" (p. 15). Silins also found that one third of the variance in student performance outcomes was a result of leader behaviors, such as establishing a shared purpose, mission, and commitment to change; improved performance; and a cohesive set of values.

Indeed, the expanded role of the principal in building school vision, which is a necessary precursor to change, has been highlighted in other recent research on transformational change in schools (Hallinger & Hausman, 1993). In fact, Leithwood (1992) has even suggested that principals who are transformational leaders should themselves articulate a vision rather than insisting that vision building become a school- and communitywide task. (Sergiovanni, 1992, warns, however, that prescribing stronger administrative leadership and increased teacher professionalism *at the same time* to cure school problems is a prescription of two antithetical concepts; in fact, "the more professionalism is emphasized, the less [principal] leadership is needed" [p. 42]. Arriving at school reform appears, then, to require a delicate balance between principal *and* teacher leadership.)

Polite (1993) has noted that the principal is the *pivotal* person in promoting the school's vision. We found that the principal is often the person who *initiates* the vision development process in shared-governance schools:

> I said, "You know, we need to bring our visions together." Everybody *wrote out his or her vision,* and one of our clerks typed it on paper bricks, and we made a foundation of the common elements from them.

I do a *workshop on vision.* That's what teaching is: It's a vision for what you can do with your life for others. A person who has a vision for shared governance is a person who sees it. They feel it. They nurture it. They build on it. And that's what we do with our vision.

I *talk* off and on informally *with the chairperson;* then when we go to a meeting, that is something we have discussed, and we just sit down and talk more about it.

In addition, shared-governance principals realize that the development of a vision requires much *time and energy;* it is an *ongoing and evolutionary process:*

It takes a *long time* to create a vision. It must be shared, not mandated, and it's not something that can happen just because it's what the principal wants.

We came up with a shared vision at a *faculty forum.* (I don't call faculty meetings anymore.) We have four or five faculty forums every year, only when we need everybody there to discuss something or take a major vote. It's usually scheduled 3 weeks ahead of time around a specific issue, and I'm only put on the agenda if I need to be.

Typically, shared-governance principals *stimulate discussion* to get the ball rolling while simultaneously ensuring that the vision that emerges is *shared:*

I ask the teachers to work through the committees and liaisons to decide, however they wish, how they want to spend the money. I say, "I'm not going to have any input in this; you and you alone are responsible." They have to work out all the turf issues and desires for more than they can get. I really just let them do it, but it's not totally without some input from me.

Our vision was *teacher generated and teacher developed.* It needs work, but it's their vision, and I'm not going to tell them what to do.

Reminders About Vision Building

The successful shared-governance principals who participated in our study demonstrated a remarkable ability to establish and maintain progress toward a *common vision* with their professional staff. We found, in many cases, that vision developed over time through a trial-and-error process. Although no simple checklist can provide a foolproof guide, the following reminders—drawn from our data—may prove helpful to educational leaders involved in developing a shared-governance vision in schools:

1. A school vision is about *instruction*—curriculum, teaching, and learning. This is the overarching, consistent focus of work in schools. Improvement efforts, driven by empowered professionals, should unerringly maintain this focus. Shared-governance principals explain:

> To paraphrase our vision: We want people who value *learning* and who value *each other.*

> Our vision is to provide an outstanding *instructional program* and to do that through a process of *empowerment.* With that in mind, we then developed a *mission* statement.

> I know this is kind of simplistic, but our vision is about whatever is best for our school, *best for our kids.* Early on, our vision was just to achieve excellence and let people find out that we are a good school. So we had to build toward that.

> Even finding the *best way to deliver instruction* might be a vision.

2. Developing a common vision is a *process,* one that is different in each school. In some schools, the development of a common vision begins as soon as shared governance is contemplated as a way of working together. In other schools, a common vision emerges later, after shared-governance structures are established, communication is buttressed, and trust is built among staff members. We found that the *activities* used to develop a vision were similar across the study schools. These activities included structured discussions in the context of teams, work with consultants on a variety of related issues (e.g., focus of work, action research, democratic processes, grouped development), short and long retreats with staff leaders and the entire faculty and staff, and other *creative and site-specific activities:*

> We had a *consultant* come in for a full 8 hours, and the school improvement team, which includes students since the third year and parents since the fourth, developed the vision statement. It includes the community, and by that we mean beyond the school walls.

I would suggest that anybody who wants to develop a vision get an *outside person* to help. We have had our bumps, our bad times, and our good times, so our consultant talked about us going through the storming phase, and we all agreed we had done that.

We went off to a nice environment and had a *consultant* help us who knows how to get a group to do a vision. We had a lot of hashing of words and ideas, and we talked about how to simplify it and how to keep it going. It was a real, open talk because we had an element of trust going.

We had a *faculty retreat* that anyone can attend. We had a *consultant* who helped us develop a mission statement when we realized that people were divided on their loyalty to the county mission statement and the local school plan, which is reflective of our mission. We really hadn't worked through that, and we needed to do some conflict resolution. We're so busy that it sometimes seems a waste of time to do that, but it was good to get everybody to focus on our beliefs and our school plan, from which we get our mission.

I said, "We're going on a *retreat* to the mountains, and we're going to develop our goals. Everybody who wants to can go." We put the money out, we went, and we worked. They trusted me enough to put them into groups, and we took the major elements of the school—like communication and climate and staff development—plugged in *people who had interests* in them, and stuck the others in there as well. Then we turned the *teams* loose with a lot of data that had been gathered over the years. They looked at the action research, developed a vision, and developed action plans. They were intense days, and we had a good time. The teams have pretty well stayed together for 2 years.

Each person wrote down what they believe an ideal school would look like. Then we had three staff meetings and another one with the parents.

Vision development also occurred through *informal* processes.

We come up with something we want to work on, and we sit down and talk. We just discuss what we think is most important. We don't necessarily take votes, but we come to consensus.

3. Often those who make the initial efforts to discuss working toward a common vision do so *voluntarily:*

The head of the science department was the Jefferson in the mission statement. She put it together, and the team said, "Gosh, this is great!" Then the faculty said, "Looks good." Two years after that we clarified some of it, and the team and the faculty again said, "Good."

You cannot tell a group of people, "We're going to be a shared-governance school, and we have to suddenly just start to live it." You *call groups together* and say, "You know, we need . . ." and "How many of you would be interested in working on . . . ?"

We had a *couple of people* who were interested in staff development and wanted to be on the vision team. *They pulled in* three or four other people they felt they could work with, and now we have spent a chunk of money on staff development, $125,000 in 6 years.

We suggest that volunteer leadership teams include organizational consultants and futurists with experience and a style conducive to handling school innovation "on the fly." Lonnquist and King (1993) described a school that attempted to develop a professional community and to become a model school of the future. The school failed to adequately develop and clarify its vision, which included preparing lifelong learners and citizens, increasing student choice and involvement in program design, and professionalizing the role of teachers. Without a method for open discussion and input from staff and the school council, without a meaningful and common interpretation of the vision, and without a continuous process to improve it, a professional community failed to develop. Facing a formidable challenge, and seeing themselves as articulating an "almost spiritual" quest, team members

did not realize the importance of or the way to orchestrate the drama, were overwhelmed with the everyday theater of [the school], and alternated between inaction and reverting to an autocratic leadership model that was not in sync with their stated vision nor conducive to the development of professional community. (Lonnquist & King, 1993, p. 24)

4. A school vision is usually put in *writing:*

We have a *vision statement, strategic plan, goals, objectives,* our *building recommendations,* and now we have developed *action plans* and put them in place.

I know the Food and Drug Administration and other regulatory agencies wouldn't love it, and it wouldn't be their approach, but we have developed the experimental vehicle, and we've already put it on the road. We haven't worked out all the kinks, and we continue to talk with people about the vision, but in order to get the vehicle moving we have a vision and a mission statement *on paper.* We didn't have time to get it perfect.

We are part of Project Achievement, and the whole idea of looking at who you are and your mission statement grew out of it. We used that information, our climate survey, our analysis of our strengths and weaknesses, information from the sessions we had with liaison groups, and the accreditation visit report to talk about what it was we were all about. We actually *wrote down* what we believe in and what it is that we want to see and hear and feel about our school. I'm talking about the whole staff. It was just ideas at first, lists of things. And then we looked at the common things, like everybody would be respected. We then *wrote* a mission statement and signed it. We have a disciplined environment where each person is respected and cared about and where children know we believe they can learn and achieve.

It's a *long statement.* I'd like it to be shorter, but I don't know if the teachers will agree with me.

The county says you have to turn in your *local school plan,* but not your belief statement and your mission statement. We have all three.

In part, a school vision may be simply *"understood":*

Part of our vision *isn't written down* anywhere, but in talking with people you would get a pretty good understanding that we want the best instructional program.

Shared-governance faculties usually express their agreement with a common vision by signing off or even voting to *support* the vision. Dissenters are given the opportunity to discuss their concerns, which may lead to revisions.

We have a mission statement *posted on the wall* of every classroom and in a lot of other places on this campus. It was developed and *voted on* by the faculty and revised once through the shared-governance process.

If somebody says, "Wait a minute, I don't want to go that way," we can *talk about it.* We haven't gotten to the point of voting yet in the 4 years we've been doing shared governance.

Finally, principals in our study noted the occasional conflicts emerging when the school's vision diverges from the district's overall goals and vision; in some cases—and with varying levels of success—principals sought waivers from policies they found to be antithetical to their efforts.

(See Figure 6.1 for an example of a shared-governance high school's *vision* statement and *goals.*)

5. Once developed, the vision becomes the *criterion of success,* a way to measure progress toward established goals:

> People who realize their vision are the ones who *keep it in front of them* all the time. It drives them. They handle it almost like a *precious jewel.* And you know, you wouldn't take something that is precious to you and not nurture it. *You keep it alive.*

> I asked the instructional advisory council to review the mission statement and to *document the actual evidence, empirical evidence, of achievements.* I initiated that because I view this as a democracy, and as citizens we can and should collect data anytime we choose to.

> If I feel uncomfortable, *I'll do a little study,* a little nosing around. We have this beautiful mission statement that uses this word, "community," . . . I said to all these people, "I can't seem to find evidence that we really have a community. We say we believe in community, but maybe the evidence shows we need to look at that." I do give them an idea of what community means to me, but I don't want to lead them.

> If we believe that all students can learn, but then when we're talking to parents we say, "I've done all I can do," *are we enacting that vision?*

6. Vision development is never static; rather, it is *ongoing* and responsive to the changing environment of the school. This was a characteristic of all the schools in our study:

> [Vision] is something you have to *keep working on* and checking. It is not something that just happens.

> We *revisit* our vision in our June meeting, and we say where we've been, where we are, and where we are going. That helps us keep focused.

> We *review* our vision every couple years, so this is our year to do that. You have to because that's what school renewal is all about. Logically, we know that every time we get 100 more kids it changes

---

**OUR VISION FOR CEDAR
CREEK HIGH SCHOOL IS . . .**

Cedar Creek High School is a diverse community in which each person values people and learning. We challenge and inspire each other toward intellectual and personal growth in a safe, nurturing environment.

Goals

1. To *create and implement action plans* designed to foster collaboration throughout the school community (i.e., teacher-to-teacher, teacher-to-student, teacher-to-parent, teacher-to-administrator collaboration)
2. To *explore alternative methods of school organization* to meet the needs of the diverse community
3. To offer opportunities to *increase understanding and valuing* of self and each other
4. To *promote student ownership* of the learning process
5. To *maintain a safe, supportive environment*

Figure 6.1. A Shared-Governance High School's Vision Statement and Goals

all our school dynamics. Our *demands are different,* so we have to review our vision.

Our vision . . . needs to be continually revisited and checked again because all of us are growing and changing all the time.

We *revisit* our vision and mission statements *every year.* We hand it out and say, "Is this still what we believe in? Is there anything we want to add or take out?"

Our vision statement is 2 years old. We probably *need to revisit* that statement; as our philosophy evolved, so too should our vision statement. It should not be a static thing; it should grow with us.

Our vision has remained basically the same, and we haven't had a big push to change it. We do go back to it *periodically*—for example, in discussing how to talk with community members more.

This year we are going to work on our vision a little differently. We're going to meet in June instead of August; that will give us all summer to work on things, some biggies that are going on.

7. *Collaboration* to achieve a school's vision stems from true commitment; this is vastly different from coordination and cooperation. Collaboration is the result of collegial efforts to achieve shared goals:

> It has to be something that is wanted *by all the people* on the staff.

> You see *how many people* we have involved in this process. I mean, it just goes on and on.

> I try to disseminate information as best as I can, but obviously it's going to be a learning process. *But everyone has their hands in* it, and things go more toward equality than toward infighting.

> We invited *students and parents* to be a part of building a vision. Some of the team for school improvement members suggested that. The chair of TSI [Team for Student Improvement] is usually a teacher, but it could be a parent or a student.

Confounding the Vision

Peterson and Solsrud's 1993 study of restructured schools found that a sustained sense of shared mission and purpose can foster deep collegial ties, reduce dysfunctional conflict, and heighten the focus on reform. However, research confirms the existence of pitfalls along the path toward achieving a vision. Remember,

1. *Leading toward a vision requires establishing ways to maintain a focus on instructional issues.* A recent study by Bondy, Ross, and Webb (1994) found that most of the restructured schools they studied were unable to pursue a mission despite having articulated mission statements. Such schools focused on developing solutions to procedural problems rather than proceeding in a clear overall direction. These problems included questions of relationships among governing bodies, how decisions are made, who serves on the council and how its chair is chosen, how people in the school are kept abreast of council activities, and who is responsible for follow-through and negotiations with the district. The researchers found that these procedural governance issues consumed enough time to keep schools from confronting their instructional mission. The school's instruc-

tional mission must be understood and shared by community stakeholders as well.

2. *Leading toward a vision is usually about shared leadership.* Reitzug (1995) suggests that if principals have a vision incongruent with the vision of teachers, they have several strategic choices: being autocratic and dictating direction, honoring the teachers' voice at the expense of their own beliefs, resigning from the position to seek an environment more compatible with their beliefs, or trying to "sell" the teachers on their direction. Some of these strategies, however, amount to what Reitzug calls "an underhanded way of accomplishing one's own agenda" (p. 10), a matter of control and manipulation. When leaders feel that they have a duty to convince others of their beliefs, Sergiovanni (1991) writes, "The test of moral leadership . . . is whether the competence, well-being, and independence of the follower is enhanced" (p. 324) and whether the "right methods" (e.g., teacher empowerment) have inappropriately been substituted for "good results" (p. 329).

3. *Leading toward a vision is about* honest *and* thoughtful *deliberation.* Educators must avoid the danger of moving too quickly to consensus or allowing consensus to "mask tensions and create an illusion of community" (Capper, 1993, p. 17).

Defining a vision, working toward it, and sustaining related efforts is a profound challenge. As one principal said, "It's really hard, but it's worth it." We now know that this work has a *symbolic or nonmaterial dimension* that provides meaning, identity, and "we-ness" for the people in a school.

References

Bondy, E., Ross, D., & Webb, R. (1994, April). *The dilemmas of school restructuring and improvement.* Paper presented at the annual meeting of the American Educational Research Association, New Orleans, LA.

Brown, D. F. (1994, April). *Experiencing shared leadership: Teachers' reflections.* Paper presented at the annual meeting of the American Educational Research Association, New Orleans, LA.

Capper, C. A. (Ed.). (1993). *Educational administration in a pluralistic society.* Albany: State University of New York Press.

Chenoweth, T., & Kushman, J. (1993, April). *Courtship and school restructuring: Building early commitment to school change for at-risk students.*

Paper presented at the annual meeting of the American Educational Research Association, Atlanta, GA.

Conley, D. T. (1991). Lessons from laboratories in school restructuring and site-based decision making. *Oregon School Study Council Bulletin, 34*(7), 1-61.

Goldman, P., Dunlap, D. M., & Conley, D. T. (1993). Facilitative power and nonstandardized solutions to school site restructuring. *Educational Administration Quarterly, 29*(1), 69-92.

Hallinger, P., & Hausman, C. (1993). The changing role of the principal in a school of choice. In J. Murphy & P. Hallinger (Eds.), *Restructuring schooling: Learning from ongoing efforts* (pp. 114-142). Newbury Park, CA: Corwin.

Leithwood, K. A. (1992). The move toward transformational leadership. *Educational Leadership, 49*(5), 8-12.

Lonnquist, M. P., & King, J. A. (1993, April). *Changing the tire on a moving bus: Barriers to the development of professional community in a new teacher-led school.* Paper presented at the annual meeting of the American Educational Research Association, Atlanta, GA.

Miles, M. B., & Ekholm, M. (1991, April). *Will new structures stay restructured?* Paper presented at the annual meeting of the American Educational Research Association, Chicago.

Peterson, K., & Solsrud, C. (1993, April). *Leadership in restructuring schools: Six themes on the worklives of principals and teachers.* Paper presented at the annual meeting of the American Educational Research Association, Atlanta, GA.

Polite, M. M. (1993, April). *Leadership and change: Working toward a paradigm shift.* Paper presented at the annual meeting of the American Educational Research Association, Atlanta, GA.

Reitzug, U. C. (1995). *Diversity, power, and influence: Multiple perspectives on the ethics of school leadership.* Unpublished manuscript, University of Wisconsin—Milwaukee.

Sergiovanni, T. J. (1991). *The principalship: A reflective practice perspective* (2nd ed.). Boston: Allyn & Bacon.

Sergiovanni, T. J. (1992). Why we should seek substitutes for leadership. *Educational Leadership, 49*(5), 41-45.

Silins, H. C. (1994, April). *Leadership characteristics that make a difference to schools.* Paper presented at the annual meeting of the American Educational Research Association, New Orleans, LA.

7

Bull's Eye

Maintaining an Instructional Focus

A sustained and undeviating focus on student learning can be considered a core characteristic of professional community.
—Kruse (1995, p. 8)

Shared-governance schools must have strong norms, collective beliefs, and values that reflect the notion that children can learn and that educators can provide school environments that support student achievement. A focus on the choices that affect learning is the essence of professional action (Darling-Hammond & Goodwin, 1993). Professional communities are identified by progress toward such goals as reflective dialogue, deprivatization of practice, focus on student learning, collaboration, and shared values (Louis & Kruse, 1995). Indeed, teachers find dignity in meaningful participation in schoolwide decisions about teaching and learning (Kruse, 1995).

Kirby and Bogotch (1995) developed a model for school empowerment based on moral ideas. These researchers found that the processes of collaboration, experimentation, reflection, continuous learning, and focusing on children contributed to a district's success toward change and innovation. In this district, the overarching belief was that *all children can learn and that the school system had the responsibility to ensure that all children would learn.* One administrator interviewed by Kirby and Bogotch noted, "[Once teachers are] empowered, they see they can make a difference in children's lives, and then we have a change in the culture, and then we have a change in the classroom."

Instructional Leadership

Kasten, Short, and Jarmin (1988) found that the most powerful feature of a successful Midwestern middle school, which was newly organized into teaching teams, was its focus on children. The total operation of the school, its slogan, and its core values focused on the rights and responsibilities of children and the opportunities the school could provide for them. And, as others have found (e.g., Mills, 1990), the instructional leadership role of the principal plays a key role in the school's ability to focus on instruction.

Having participatory governance structures (e.g., school site councils) alone does not guarantee that schools will focus on *improving instruction* (Peterson & Solsrud, 1993; Wohlstetter, Smyer, & Mohrman, 1994). Principals must be instructional leaders. An active process of school restructuring provides an agreed-on direction that focuses talk among educators on teaching and learning. Principals can play a significant role in facilitating restructuring processes.

Getting on With the Business of Schools

Although it is often argued that an open process that includes different perspectives increases the creativity and productivity of school-based decision making, some leaders tend to stress *collegiality* (or other factors) over academic *substance* (that is, teaching and learning). Hayes, Glickman, and Allen (1995) indicate that teachers have different views of empowerment. In the *personal* view, empowerment is associated with more pay, a larger classroom, greater autonomy, and better working conditions. The *relational* view stresses pleasant colleagues, fewer work impediments and hassles, fewer rules, better communication, and knowing who will be involved and how. With the *extensional* view, empowerment is related to having real and substantive control over one's destiny and in being able to contribute to the greater good of the school.

In related work, Kruse (1995, pp. 12-13) describes three possible types of relationships among teachers as they prepare to focus on student learning:

1. *Cooperative relationships*—Teachers discuss students more and learning less.
2. *Collegial relationships*—Teachers hold rudimentary dialogues related to classroom practice and student performance (e.g., lesson plans, student work expectations and behavior).
3. *Collaborative relationships*—Teachers discuss the development of practice and process skills; they create shared understandings from complex and confused information.

True collaborative relationships increase the possibility of having "richly substantive discourse" (Little, 1990, p. 522) about the business of schools: teaching and learning.

Both the Hayes et al. (1995) and the Kruse (1995) frameworks are useful tools in describing and discussing different viewpoints on empowerment and types of working relationships, and in beginning the process of empowering teachers and improving instruction.

How Principals Facilitate Focus

Effective shared-governance principals help teachers to focus improvement efforts on teaching and learning (Keedy & Finch, 1994). Bondy, Ross, and Webb (1994) found that only one of the six schools they studied had substantially restructured. In this school the principal performed the key leadership act of providing many *opportunities* for participants to study and discuss teaching and learning. She also kept the *focus* on the school's mission, which was to help all students learn.

Wohlstetter et al. (1994) indicated that the actively restructuring schools they studied concentrated on instructional improvement by a variety of means. These included developing mechanisms to generate interactions about curriculum and instruction, providing cross-role training of teachers, facilitating information flow across classrooms and grade levels, and enabling teachers to work together on teams, subcommittees, and councils. Such forms of interaction created a sense of community and provided an agreed-upon direction that *maintained the focus on teaching and learning.*

The exemplary principals we investigated encouraged an instructional focus among teachers in a variety of ways—most important, by talking, making suggestions, and as several principals reported, by consistently reinforcing the focus.

> I *talk constantly* about looking at things that we can do to improve.

> I think we are able to stay focused on instruction because it's one of the things that *I keep in front of them.* It's about why we are here, and that comes down to, "We're here for the kids."

> Our instructional initiative is writing. We feel that if you can write, you can read. And we always say, "The more you read, the more you know." Some of the kids even know it because *I say it so much*!

> At every single meeting we have, the vision statement goes up first. We always recite it, our little mantra. It goes up on the overhead and sits on the table. It is what we believe. All of our decisions must concentrate on that vision, which is about *learning.*

> I try to keep focused by saying that *my feeling is that instruction is the key* to everything in the school, but I don't think that everybody has bought into that. We have a very talented, creative faculty, and they get distracted. For example, we had this huge Hansel and Gretel production with a special grant and a dance group. It was really special, but it wasn't done as an interdisciplinary unit; if it had been, it could have involved everyone. It was still magical, but it could have been even more of a learning experience.

Shared-governance principals also relied on teacher leaders, formal improvement programs, and the school vision (or mission) to help maintain a focus on instruction in their schools. The role of teacher leaders was discussed by one principal:

> We continually come back to *instruction* because we have strong leadership in the curriculum areas. Teachers meet regularly, pull people together, have course-grade meetings, and stay focused on instruction.

Another principal described the relationship between improvement programs and focus:

> One way to stay focused on instruction is by focusing on our Program for School Improvement; it's the *vehicle* for the task forces and for all the changes that are made in the school.

None of the principals we interviewed was inclined to *force* teachers to adopt an instructional focus; rather, they predicted that those teachers who were not instructionally inclined would leave or be asked to leave.

> If a teacher can't buy into what I'm trying to do, then pretty soon, just like cream rises to the top, he or she is going to feel inadequate. And either they're going to volunteer [to leave], or I am going to ask them to leave.

> If I determine in my teacher evaluations that there is a problem with a teacher not being prepared for class—staying focused on learning—I just say it.

One principal's comments highlight some of the *problems* encountered by shared-governance schools in maintaining the focus on instruction:

> We face three major problems in staying focused on instruction: Once you get involved in democratic processes, you begin to uncover problems, and you have a tendency to want to fix them in a hurry. The problem is that democracy is a slow process. The second problem is the messy desk syndrome: You can't decide which piece of paper to deal with because there are so many in front of you. The third thing that makes it difficult to focus is negative people. With every issue there is somebody throwing stones.

Moving From Trivial to Critical Decisions

Kirby (1991) found that newly empowered faculties tend to begin their deliberations by addressing managerial and housekeeping issues. For instance, the faculties she studied dealt with concerns about student discipline policies, duty schedules, and parking and faculty lounges; they addressed instructional matters (e.g., staff development, program planning, at-risk programs) later. Kirby's findings are consistent with those of Glickman (1993) on the League of Professional Schools. Glickman warns,

> The work of schools is teaching and learning for the higher purpose of productive democratic citizenship. When school community members spend most of their time on administrative, managerial, and adult convenience/congenial activities, they lose their sense of purpose. (p. 32)

Table 7.1, constructed from the work of the League of Professional Schools, shows the various focuses of decisions, ranging from those with no impact on learning to those with a comprehensive impact on learning. In our study, we discovered a tendency of school faculties to emphasize low-impact decisions during the early stages of implementing shared governance. However, one principal had a particularly positive experience in developing an instructional focus:

> Early on, you focus quickly on the *noninstructional issues* and get them out of the way. After that it's pretty smooth sailing. It's easy then to stay focused on instruction. The Instructional Leadership team deals only with schoolwide instructional issues. If a noninstructional issue comes up now, it's directed to the appropriate party—an administrator, the head of the English department or the math department, or to whomever.

Most of the principals we studied, however, disclosed that student *management/discipline* continually interferes with maintaining a focus on education.

> Our faculty confronts *challenges* to staying focused on instruction, such as the everyday functioning of the school, student management, and the facts of life in a school as big as ours. If 5% of our kids are screwing around and giving us a hard time, we spend 80% of our time on 10% of the kids, you know. But the teachers said, "If the administrators are managing the kids, that means we don't have control; we want to manage the students." So the teachers decided on a schoolwide five- or six-step process to follow, but to implement those steps you take time away from your other kids. It eats you up, just like the two [middle school] kids smoking marijuana; that took one lady [an administrator] all day to resolve, so her other 450 kids did not get her attention at all that day. Well, one in your classroom can take away from the other 27 just like that.

The *routine demands* of school life, special interest groups, and the district office also continually threaten the school's ability to develop and maintain its focus on education.

> You've always got the *demands of life*. I have to be real honest: There are some days . . . ! The visitor and the auditor were coming this morning, two assistants are at another meeting, and one assistant is at the Capitol. If all that hadn't been happening, I would have taken the day off. Seriously, just for my wife and me.

TABLE 7.1 Focus of Governance: Educational Impact

Zero-Impact Decisions	Minimal-Impact Decisions	Core-Impact Decisions	Comprehensive-Impact Decisions
Parking spaces	Textbook adoption	Curriculum	School budget
Lunchroom supervision	Parent programs	Staff development	Hiring of personnel
Faculty lounge	In-service days	Coaching	Deployment of personnel
Sunshine fund	Small budgets	Instructional programs	Personnel evaluation
Adult recreation	Discipline policy	Student assessment	
Bus duties	Instructional budget		
Refreshments			

SOURCE: From *Renewing America's Schools: A Guide for School-Based Action,* p. 33, by C. D. Glickman, 1993, San Francisco: Jossey-Bass. Reprinted with permission.

We've had sick children, and we haven't had time to spend with one another. Keeping 142 adults focused is tough when you've got so many other demands.

We get distracted from instruction by *individual issues*—you know, like little special-interest groups that want to come before the leadership council with whatever issue is bugging them that week. It may not be instructionally related (like the parking lot issue). *Those things are always there,* and they don't ever totally go away, although they're a lot more in the background than they used to be. People get upset about something, and they want to make it a faculty issue.

It bothers me that we're spending *more time on management decisions* than on instructional decisions. We are becoming expert at a governing system, at solving problems, generating solutions, working together as a team, but our leadership team is becoming the catchall for central-office, system-level programs. It's a dumping ground for informational meetings, policy updates, budget revisions, and the superintendent's objectives. The central office is trying to mold us and tell us what we're supposed to be doing. But our team really gravitates toward instructional issues, and our shared-governance charter says we deal with instructional issues. We're not being permitted to do so. There's a group of principals in the district that just met to talk about this very issue, finding ourselves pulled off track all the time. Here's the newest one: They're installing a computer at my school to monitor the energy needs for every classroom in the building; that's my new function! The superintendent feels that with site-based management, he is mandated to get the management of the schools out into the schools, but the decision making is still handled downtown.

Shared-governance principals also described a multiplicity of *other issues* that sabotage substantive instructional work.

The *extraneous things* make it tough to stay focused. If a faculty member has a terminally ill parent at home, they're not going to be involved. The other part is the naysayers. Phil Schlecty says you've got trailblazers, pioneers, settlers, stay-at-homers, and saboteurs. The saboteurs just yak, yak, yak about "The administration's already decided that" or "You're just a puppet," and it's hard to overcome that.

Teachers have *issues* all the time that have nothing to do with instruction. I remind them that grade-level managers are the people to talk to about managerial concerns [those concerns that are not instruction based]. The instructional council takes care of all instructional things.

Sometimes there are *so many things* going through the pipes that we have to meet for an hour to make sure we all fully understand what we're doing. You really can't get into anything in a half hour, and I have a problem with taking teachers out of the classroom to have study-group meetings or instructional council meetings. So we meet after school.

Given the difficulty of maintaining an instructional focus in decision making in shared-governance schools, Kirby's (1991, pp. 14-15) propositions are *instructive* with regard to effective practice:

1. School improvement teams will be more likely to address issues of greater significance when *minor faculty concerns are resolved first,* thereby fostering trust in the process and facilitating a more professional culture.

2. School leadership teams will be more likely to address issues of greater significance when they are able to focus their own work

through *formal structures* for goal setting, determining agendas, and reaching decisions.

3. School leadership teams will be more likely to address issues of greater significance when more people are *involved* in prioritizing concerns and when those people declare a stake in the outcomes.

4. School leadership teams will be more likely to address issues of greater significance when the *database* for generating concerns, alternatives, and solutions is both comprehensive and objective (such as an analysis of optimum and existing school effectiveness criteria to generate concerns or a literature review to generate alternatives).

Sources of Data for Instructional Decisions

The last proposition, about a comprehensive *database,* is especially relevant to the experiences of the principals in our study—principals who use action research and other forms of data collection and analysis to make decisions in collaboration with teachers, parents, and students. Nevertheless, effective use of data collection protocols is not easily achieved:

> We had so many different forms of information that it drove the teachers crazy. It was hectic, and you could see it in the teachers' faces. So we analyzed our writing process, and we had so many little pieces of paper, so many forms—a summary, a roster, a check form—and we said, "This is just too much." So we went back and revamped and made it more efficient, more practical. It was *too much stuff*; it was almost *blinding.*

Glickman (1993) has identified several sources of data available for school improvement: (a) *conventional* data (e.g., attendance rates, referrals, test scores, dropout rates), (b) *traditional* data (e.g., survey data, interview data, writing samples), and (c) *creative* data (e.g., student exhibits and portfolios, videotapes, performance assessments). He urges the use of *multiple* and *increasingly creative* data sources to drive shared decision-making efforts in a school. The use of a variety of sources enriches understanding of issues and illuminates paths to improvement (see Calhoun, 1994, for practical ideas about education action research).

Parental input is considered an excellent potential data source for instructional decisions in shared-governance schools. As we noted earlier, however, research on school reform has demonstrated that principals themselves may interfere with a school's ability to develop and maintain a focus on educational matters by, for example, restricting the influence of parents (and teachers) to trivial issues and to rubber-stamping administrative decisions (Malen & Ogawa, 1988). In our study, we too found that parent involvement in decision making is quite limited and, indeed, seldom addresses instructional issues (see Chapter 5 for more about parental and student involvement).

> We have writing contests, and sometimes *parents* help with it. The October contest was Harvest Moon; grade-level winners got a dinner at Red Lobster. It's a way to encourage them to write and to involve the parents. We also send newsletters and progress reports to parents.

> A challenge that we face is getting the *parents* involved in the learning process. A lot of them grew up here and think their school has always been great. They're not concerned. They really don't want to come in and get their feet wet. Some, though, will go in classrooms and do extraordinary things, wonderful things. We have a father who keeps up the whole grounds virtually by himself, and we have parents on the safety committees.

Clearly, more parental involvement in matters relating directly to student achievement is needed. Increasing parental involvement is one of the challenges of shared-governance programs designed to improve student learning.

Staying on Course

Prestine (1994) advocates constant vigilance to keep attention focused on common beliefs and shared understandings so that they become part of the routine operation of a school. One of the principals we interviewed commented that it was "easy to slip into old patterns." Another, however, discussed her school's success in maintaining a focus that is broad and extends well *beyond* instruction:

> Our focus is not just on trying to improve classroom practice. We have this other side of our efforts whereby we've tried to change

the organizational *culture* that affects instruction. It goes back to the vision.

All of the principals in our study monitor shared-governance processes and help maintain the school's focus on instructional matters. Facilitating instructional focus is central to a clear, consistent shared-governance approach to schooling. To sum up, factors that help maintain a focus on instruction—which principals considered their "number-one" responsibility—include the following:

+ Clear, shared vision/mission statements
+ Use of action research
+ Strong leadership among faculty in curriculum
+ Committees with instructional focus
+ Effective discipline policies
+ Effective instructional programs
+ Continuous evaluation and assessment
+ Collaboration among faculty
+ Collaboration with parents

And as our data point out, the primary sources of interference with maintaining an instructional focus are

+ noninstructional issues
+ lack of time
+ central-office demands
+ educators' personal problems
+ negativity and pessimism

References

Bondy, E., Ross, D., & Webb, R. (1994, April). *The dilemmas of school restructuring and improvement.* Paper presented at the annual meeting of the American Educational Research Association, New Orleans, LA.

Calhoun, E. (1994). *How to use action research in the self-renewing school.* Alexandria, VA: Association for Supervision and Curriculum Development.

Darling-Hammond, L., & Goodwin, A. L. (1993). Progress towards professionalism in teaching. In G. Cawelti (Ed.), *Challenges and achievements*

of American education: The 1993 ASCD yearbook (pp. 19-52).
Alexandria, VA: Association for Supervision and Curriculum Development.

Glickman, C. D. (1993). Renewing America's schools: A guide for school-based action. San Francisco: Jossey-Bass.

Hayes, R. L., Glickman, C. D., & Allen, L. (1995). What does it mean to be empowered? Unpublished manuscript.

Kasten, K. L., Short, P. M., & Jarmin, C. (1988, April). Using organization structures and shared leadership to enrich the professional lives of teachers: A case study in self-managing groups. Paper presented at the annual meeting of the American Educational Research Association, New Orleans, LA.

Keedy, J. L., & Finch, A. M. (1994). Examining teacher-principal empowerment: An analysis of power. Journal of Research and Development in Education, 27(3), 162-175.

Kirby, P. C. (1991, April). Shared decision making: Moving from concerns about restrooms to concerns about classrooms. Paper presented at the annual meeting of the American Educational Research Association, Chicago.

Kirby, P. C., & Bogotch, I. E. (1995, April). Empowerment and information utilization within a restructuring school district. Paper presented at the annual meeting of the American Educational Research Association, San Francisco.

Kruse, S. D. (1995, April). Teachers' reflective work: School-based support structures. Paper presented at the annual meeting of the American Educational Research Association, San Francisco.

Little, J. W. (1990). The persistence of privacy: Autonomy and initiative in teachers' professional relations. Teachers College Record, 91(4), 509-536.

Louis, K. S., & Kruse, S. D. (Eds.). (1995). Professionalism and community: Perspectives from urban schools. Thousand Oaks, CA: Corwin.

Malen, B., & Ogawa, R. T. (1988). Professional-patron influence on site-based governance councils: A confounding case study. Educational Evaluation and Policy Analysis, 10(4), 251-270.

Mills, G. E. (1990). A consumer's guide to school improvement (Trends and Issues series, No. 4). Eugene, OR: ERIC Clearinghouse on Educational Management. (ERIC Document Reproduction Service No. ED 313-800)

Peterson, K., & Solsrud, C. (1993, April). Leadership in restructuring schools: Six themes on the worklives of principals and teachers. Paper presented at the annual meeting of the American Educational Research Association, Atlanta, GA.

Prestine, N. A. (1994). Ninety degrees from everywhere: New understanding of the principal's role in a restructuring essential school. In J. Murphy (Ed.), Reshaping the principalship: Insights from transformational reform efforts (pp. 123-154). Thousand Oaks, CA: Corwin.

Wohlstetter, P., Smyer, R., & Mohrman, S. A. (1994). New boundaries for school-based management: The high involvement model. Educational Evaluation and Policy Analysis, 16(3), 268-286.

8

The Inner Experience

It can be frightening to leap into the unknown with no maps to follow and few reliable guides.
—Clift, Johnson, Holland, & Veal (1992, p. 906)

Movement toward teacher professionalism does not signal the death of the principalship. But the principal's job is changing. The power of principals to lead through fear, domination, and coercion is lessening. Those who need those powers are endangered.
—King & Kerchner (1991, p. 10)

The key roles of the principal in shared governance include managing the change process (Mills, 1990), providing an increased level of instructional leadership (Osterman, 1989), and managing group processes (Schmuck & Runkel, 1985). However, such significant role changes may produce loss of control and uncertainty, fear of failure, self-doubts about competence and ability to succeed, impatience, frustration, and loss of identity (Bredeson, 1995). These effects are not limited to the principal; Duttweiler and Mutchler (1990), among others, have noted that many educators in restructured schools experience difficulties associated with accepting new roles and responsibilities, losing power, lacking necessary skills, lacking trust, and fear of risk taking.

This chapter describes some of the profound inner changes—changes that our study principals experienced as challenging, rewarding, and even spiritual—that resulted from their involvement

117

in shared governance. After all is said and done, these changes are experienced as inspirational; as one principal stated, "The fire is back!"

Challenges

Am I Needed?

Henderson and Hawthorne (1993) write:

The evolution from power over to shared power is a complex developmental journey that requires a form of transitional leadership in which facilitation of sharing is fostered and the vision of participative democracy is kept central. The desire to retreat to the comfort of familiar bureaucratic structures and procedures to obtain closure or a sense of movement reasserts itself frequently in our work. For many, the uncertainty and messiness of democratic processes evoke a strong sense of vulnerability. (p. 10)

Principals involved in school reform programs such as shared governance often experience a substantial amount of role conflict and related anxiety and uncertainty (Alexander, 1992). They may, for example, wonder if they are needed and even feel hurt at being excluded from decision-making processes:

You always wonder if *you're really needed*. You think, "Well, do they really need me here, or do they even want me here?" A lot of times you start to question, "Could this place just run without me?" But if it can run without me, then I know I'm doing the right thing, honestly. But then a parent calls, one who won't talk with the teacher anymore, and I know I'm needed.

Have you ever *wondered whether you're really needed*? I know that I'm really needed. The county and the community look to me as the head of the school, as the one to assure them that we are being legal and all that kind of stuff. I think it's more of a legal role because I delineate parameters for decisions. But I don't think the teachers always realize how much they need me; sometimes they think that if I was out of the picture, they wouldn't have all these limitations. They don't always understand that it's not me making up the rules. Also, now I have more of a community relations role, and I spend more time on community involvement. In the past I might not have been able to be proactive enough to let the community know where our problems are.

> They even said *they didn't think I needed to be at all of the grade-level meetings,* and it kind of *hurt my feelings.* I mean it really did. But they said it wasn't at all personal, but it was just that I didn't need to hear every little thing they complain about and that if it is really important, I would hear it . . . but I didn't think of myself as being their boss. I just think I'm one of them, and I think that they should be able to complain and gripe and not worry about me getting upset with them. Some people just can't get over me being the principal. I understand it, but I don't like it. So I said, "Fine," and now if I have something to share, I ask to be on the agenda.

The strain engendered by the significant role changes that accompany school reform may be mitigated, at least partially, by *cognitive restructuring.* Bredeson (1995) found that this was the primary coping strategy used by principals to reduce role strain. In addition, personal factors such as locus of control, leadership style, capacity for growth, tolerance for ambiguity, patience, and interpersonal communication skills helped to moderate the adverse effects of role strain. Various forms of support from superintendents (e.g., trust, time, funds) also helped to alleviate role strain. The principals we interviewed emphasized the benefits of becoming a *partner* in the educational enterprise:

> I'm growing, learning to become more of a *partner,* learning to become more democratic. I'm certainly not there yet. You get a lot more accomplished working with a group than trying to work by yourself.

> The old way was more lonely, much more separate. My position of power *separated* me from the staff. I had all the authority and all the responsibility, and I'll tell you it was a much simpler concept.

Clift et al. (1992) offer the following suggestions for principals confronting role strain within changing school contexts:

1. Shared leadership for schoolwide initiatives is not a naturally occurring phenomenon. Principals must *signal* to others that they are willing to listen, to respect teachers' decisions, and to support action on initiatives led by teachers. This will promote consensus and reduce ambiguity.

2. School and district *context* should not be ignored. For example, teachers working at different levels may have very different expectations regarding their authority to make decisions.
3. Working together is a dynamic process. Educators must be willing to *tolerate ambiguity* as roles change, and they must communicate that willingness to each other.
4. Change processes are fragile. *Time* demands, in particular, must be discussed early in any change effort and revisited frequently to ensure no one is being left out because of time constraints.

What About Power, Control, Inadvertent Domination, and Contrived Collegiality?

The espoused theory of teacher leadership will be undermined if [administrators'] theories in action stress teacher compliance as opposed to creative risk taking. (Clift et al., 1992, p. 906)

Although democratic participation is a vehicle for greater professional control, some principals fear the erosion of their traditional authority, and this fear can produce tension between them and teachers. In his study of the principal's role in implementing shared decision making, Smith (1995) investigated one principal who initially reported that he fulfilled the role of facilitator by "giving permission" to the faculty to take on decision-making responsibilities. Two years later, this principal realized that a true shared-governance leadership required specialized training and expertise and the ability to *teach others* to take responsibility and make decisions.

The approach to leadership employed by the principal whom Smith (1995) studied could be characterized as "inadvertent domination" (Reitzug & Cross, 1994). To illustrate, principals may inadvertently dominate faculty deliberations through the frequency and length of their participation. This form of domination may also be produced by traditional expectations of self and of others and the principal's possession of knowledge and information not available to other team members (e.g., legal and financial matters). Thus, under the guise of democracy and the rhetoric of devolution of power (which attempts to recognize the practitioner's experience and wisdom), bureaucratic structures and traditional patterns of power relationships may persist.

Real change may be circumscribed, and the reality of principal control and teacher compliance may prevail. Teachers do not engage in "matters of the mind" but instead make "devastating compromises in order to survive" (Smyth, 1992, p. 274). Real change may be further sabotaged by leaders of "stony indifference" who have an inability and even hostility with regard to reflective educational practice (Gibboney, 1990, p. 10). Several of the shared-governance principals we studied revealed, sometimes unwittingly, their inclination to *control* others.

> Even though I say that I am participatory and a supporter, I feel that in some way I still have some *tendency to control* in me. And I have to let go.

> My philosophy is that you're going to come in and give 125%, or you're not going to be here. That sounds hard and cold, but that's the way I had to approach leadership. . . . In 1975, I went into a situation where I had to take *control*. I had to get rid of people who didn't have a commitment to the school, and I had to suspend a lot of kids, and I had to get the parents' attention. It took years to assemble a staff I felt comfortable with and could work with.

> Accountability is a major part of my approach—*my being accountable* for the delivery of the curriculum, the instructional methods, and the results we get.

In contrast, other principals readily accepted the redistribution of *power* that comes with shared decision making:

> I am not turned on by *suppressing* others, forcing compliance.

> The power brokers have died out now. *Power is so diffuse* that it's difficult for one person or group to dominate anything. Power is spread out like crazy. Part of the shared-governance process is to give power to the folks, and it comes back to you in a mutual way that you can't stop.

> Because I'm not controlling everything, the school is actually in better control than it ever was. We talk about all *being in the same soup,* being in this together. There's *more power to share,* not less, and the pie has grown bigger.

> I have less power now, and it's harder on me. I have more to do, but I also have more *depth* as a leader.

> I said, "There are no parameters, no guidelines, *no limits*. You tell
> me what you want to do with the schedule." I just had to let it
> happen and be willing to live with the consequences. That's the key
> to the whole thing.

Remarkably, this *redistribution of power* assuages the *loneliness*
that principals experienced as traditional leaders.

> The difference is that I don't have to sit down and ponder what I
> should do for this school. Instead, I can pull the council together. I
> don't have to do things *by myself* anymore. . . . We're in it together.

We should mention that the successful principals we interviewed
never mandated shared governance for their schools. Our data
indicate that they are quite aware, for example, that imposing
collaboration and collegiality could undermine the communication
and trust necessary to establish viable relationships. Hargreaves
(1991) has found that "contrived" collegial relationships—imposed,
administratively regulated, compulsory, and fixed in time and
space—frequently fail to produce authentic collegiality in schools.
Conley (1988) notes, "Even today, there are plenty of schools that
may fit the criteria of school site management, but they are managed
by one person: the principal" (p. 2). Such schools represent shared
governance in *form* only (Bolin, 1989).

Major Rewards

As leaders of leaders, teachers of teachers, as the teacher who is
"one among equals," effective shared-governance principals find the
work rewarding on various levels. They feel open, alive, self-aware,
and motivated, and are able to behave in ways consistent with
personal values. For them, *the fire is back!*

> Personally and professionally, [shared governance] has given me a
> great sense of *satisfaction*. I really believe in the process, and I have
> enjoyed it. I like watching people grow. I like change when it is
> needed. I like to be on the cutting edge, in uncharted territory; I
> would have enjoyed being an explorer! When you have shared
> governance, you move forward on instructional matters and cur-
> riculum. I say that as a point of pride. I also enjoy sharing ideas
> about shared-governance because I have a bit of the philosopher in

me. I've blocked out a couple hours here and there to engage in conversations and workshops with educators from this country and Canada; it's fun to deal with real-life issues. I teach graduate classes for future administrators and talk about how we practice shared governance in our school. It's a real-world model of shared governance!

It's personally *rewarding* in a lot of respects. I'm doing something that I really, really believe in. Through shared governance for school improvement, I have had the opportunity to share ideas and work with a lot of people. I was one of the people who helped get the first state conference on shared governance set up, and I absolutely loved it! It's an extension of what I'm doing academically in my doctoral program—reading about participative decision making and writing papers about it. It's *unifying* for a lot of people.

Involvement in shared governance has dramatic effects on principals' *motivation to work:*

I had gotten real discouraged over two or three things, and I finally reached the point that everybody reaches in their career. It just hit me: Is this what I want to do for the rest of my life? Is there something else I need to be doing? The answer came after a year of real serious struggle. This is what I am supposed to do! And I *got that fire back,* the fire I had when I was 21 and just walked out of college.

Becoming a shared-governance school has helped me in several ways. Number one, it helps me get up and come to work every day. *I'm excited!* I look forward to it! I even look forward to when breaks are over! I've always loved schools and wanted to be a principal since the first grade. My daddy used to build schools, and when I was a toddler I would go around to the new schools he was building. And I got what I wanted, to be a principal. For a few years, though, I really struggled, but now the *fire is back!*

I am so *excited* about being here. Shared governance works. It's good stuff.

Often the process of shared governance reveals the *self* of the principals—who they are as people:

I feel I've grown personally, and I *understand myself* better.

Shared governance has made me realize what some of my *strengths* are and what some of my *weaknesses* are. It makes me know better who I am. For example, I do know good teaching and classroom practice, but when it comes down to specific content and kids, I don't get involved, and I don't pretend I know something I don't. Also, one of my weaknesses is that I don't like crowds. When I leave here, you'll find me at home or on the tennis court or hitting a golf ball, and the only public part of me is the actual job. This job forces me to be in the public's eye, but I'm just not a public person. Still, I'm comfortable now with what my role is.

As I reflect on the effects of shared governance, I would have to say that I've grown more *comfortable with who I am* personally. The years of experience have taken a toll on me, and I have also grown from experience. . . . Shared governance has brought a very unique situation to me; the process has given me a *deeper sense* of who I am because it is a process in which I am personally involved.

Shared governance also demands *consistency between personal values and professional leadership:*

The staff is watching to see if you *practice what you preach,* so you've got to *internalize* it. If you break trust, it's hard to get it back. I share just as much as I possibly can and don't just make the decision. If I make the mistake of doing that on occasion, I don't lie to them. I am honest.

I know there's a lot more to it than a simple little definition, but it's hard to articulate to somebody what's within you. The teachers have to see the principal *living his / her belief* in shared governance.

I just feel good personally. This is the way schools should be run. After all, *we live in a democracy,* and we ought to make decisions together. Ultimately I feel personal satisfaction that we are doing what is best for children.

In very simple terms, it's about *knowing who you are* and what you're comfortable with. In terms of book knowledge, it's situational.

I am conscious of when I make a decision that I shouldn't have made myself, . . . when I have violated shared-governance principles. I have grown professionally because *I have the mind-set* to notice immediately. Then I go back to the faculty and say, "You're not going to believe what I did." If anyone is upset I say, "I'm sorry."

All schools in the district were mandated to enact site-based management, but I was *predisposed* to shared governance already, and I had a mandate from the staff and community. It crushes those people who are not comfortable with it, and then it's a terrible struggle. And even for those of us who are accustomed to shared governance, we know we are still ultimately accountable for every function in the school.

Shared governance is profoundly rewarding in that it allows the principal to *grow* and to witness the *growth of others*. It provides opportunities for teachers to develop leadership expertise and flourish as self-actualized professionals.

Shared governance has helped me *grow* as a leader, helped me to create a whole new vision of what leadership is, to open doors, to be more inclusive. It's so much *fun to watch people grow as leaders*. It's a tremendous feeling. The power base is broadened, and I'm less lonely.

When I came to this school, I was warned how difficult this one teacher is to work with. . . . She has grown with shared governance, and we have recognized her for her excellent leadership ability. I begged her to let me nominate her for the leadership team, but she said she's not ready yet. She has tremendous leadership potential, and it's just *like flowers in a garden when you see them bloom*! It makes me feel so good!

More teachers from our school than any other school in the state presented at the middle school conference. We already knew they were experts, but they realized it even more so through the *development of their leadership potential*.

The shared-governance process takes a lot of time, but it allows *my personality, my style, to come out*. I would have been uncomfortable with an autocratic role. I am also making professional training opportunities available to teachers so they learn how to be leaders and how to make decisions. *They're all leaders,* you know, not just the principal.

What you really get from shared governance is *strength*. It has cultivated some real creative teachers and secretaries and brought them into that brain trust. I've enjoyed seeing what has come out of efforts from the ground up when people have been empowered to get involved. It's a *creative synergy*.

Teachers are more *committed* to their jobs, and their personal and professional lives are linked. We have gotten to know each other better, and we have become more understanding of each other. They are even more understanding of my personal concerns; they notice if I've been meeting with them all day and say that I must be tired, with all the other responsibilities I have. They see me more as a *peer* now.

Being part of the shared-governance movement has given me *an opportunity* to be exposed to a lot of the new trends and practical things that are happening. I've been *sharing* so much, especially about the middle level of schooling, and now I have no desire to go

anywhere else. Now I *encourage* the teachers to go out and be
involved in things. We've learned that you can always bring something back to your school to improve it when you go out.

Subsidiary Awards

Principals revealed additional rewarding experiences when they
reflected on their career, contemplated their attitude toward work,
and thought about personal conversions. These experiences included
becoming a teacher of teachers, realizing benefits for one's family,
and receiving good press.

Teacher of Teachers

One principal's words mirror what all the principals we studied
experienced:

> I will tell you what I believe and what it comes down to. In my mind,
> *the shared-governance principal is the ultimate teacher.* There is
> something that is important to you, and real teachers have the
> same burning inside: We want to make a difference in the lives of
> kids, and we want to be free to do it. The great teachers are the
> ones who reach out and begin to live it. We've even had some
> converts who admit they were missing it, and they said, "Why didn't
> we do this a long time ago?" Some of them say, "This is what I
> dreamed about when I started teaching." Some people are *on fire,*
> fired up to do this.

Benefits for Family

Even a principal's family can benefit from involvement in shared
governance.

> This is a small community, and if you are the principal and you are
> successful, you have some standing in the community. I swear.
> People know me, they trust me, they call me for advice. But because
> I like to be at school, and I now *feel so good about what I am doing,*
> it has also helped my family. I have three kids, and now I have a
> focus for them, too.

> I have learned to *work smarter* because I have so many things to
> juggle and less time to do them. I'm trying to *give more time* to my
> husband and my home.

Good Press

Principals also derived rewards from public recognition and the opportunity to demonstrate their school's shared-governance approaches.

> The Association for Supervision and Curriculum Development people called us and said that they had heard that we were doing some collaborative action research and they were interested in hearing about it. They said they *wanted to come out the next week* and videotape us. The staff members were ecstatic, even though we have people in the school all the time because of our shared-governance process.

> We've gotten a lot of positive *attention* for what we're doing here, and it's been real rewarding. We got a National School of Excellence award, and that's my picture—shaking hands with Bill [President Clinton]!

The Spirituality of Shared Governance

Principals sometimes described their *collaborative work with respected professionals* as "spiritual":

> Shared governance is within you. It's *spiritual*. I hesitate to use the term *spiritual,* but in a way it is. . . . It's just in you. You either understand it or you don't. You believe in it, or you don't. You live with it every day, and then whatever you're trying to do will bring it out.

> My own *spiritual beliefs* and my *beliefs about education* are *mixed together* real tight. For me, it has to work that way. You have to have the attitude that shared governance is good for people, and you can't be arrogant. Humility is the name of the game. You've got to be humble and step aside and say, "These are the people who have done that. It wasn't me." Giving them credit is the important thing.

> There is a *spirituality* to shared governance. You know, teaching is a vision of what you can do with your life for others. It's the same with shared governance. A person who has a vision for shared governance in a school is a person who sees it. That person feels it, and nurtures it, and builds on it. People who realize their *vision* keep it in front of them at all times. It drives them. They handle it like a *precious jewel* to some extent, and you wouldn't take something that is precious to you and not nurture it, not keep it alive.

You cannot tell a group of people, "We're going to be a shared governance school" and make them have to suddenly just start to live it. You call groups together. You see who is interested in working on something. They meet. One person emerges as the natural leader, and they make the decisions on their own. I just had to let it happen and be willing to live with the consequences; that's the key to the whole thing.

All in all, we found that in spite of all the uncertainty and anxiety that result from diving into the shared-governance experience, principals are actually less lonely and very motivated. Also, principals' actions become more consistent with their beliefs and values, and their inner experience includes a spirituality that brings back "the fire" they once had but lost as educators.

References

Alexander, G. C. (1992, April). *The transformation of an urban principal: Uncertain times, uncertain roles.* Paper presented at the annual meeting of the American Educational Research Association, San Francisco.

Bolin, F. S. (1989). Empowering leadership. *Teachers College Record, 91*(1), 81-96.

Bredeson, P. V. (1995, April). *From gazing out the ivory towers to heavy lifting in the field: Empowerment through collaborative action research.* Paper presented at the annual meeting of the American Educational Research Association, San Francisco.

Clift, R., Johnson, M., Holland, P., & Veal, M. L. (1992). Developing the potential for collaborative school leadership. *American Educational Research Journal, 29*(4), 877-908.

Conley, S. C. (1988, April). *From school site management to "participatory school site management."* Paper presented at the annual meeting of the American Educational Research Association, New Orleans, LA.

Duttweiler, P. C., & Mutchler, M. (1990). *Organizing the educational system for excellence: Harnessing the energy of people.* Philadelphia: Research for Better Schools.

Gibbonney, R. (1990). *The killing field of reform.* Unpublished manuscript, University of Pennsylvania, Philadelphia.

Hargreaves, A. (1991). Contrived collegiality: The micropolitics of teacher collaboration. In J. Blase (Ed.), *The politics of life in schools* (pp. 46-72). Newbury Park, CA: Sage.

Henderson, J. G., & Hawthorne, R. D. (1993, April). *The dialectics of creating professional development schools: Reflections on work in progress.* Paper presented at the annual meeting of the American Educational Research Association, Atlanta, GA.

King, B., & Kerchner, C. T. (1991, April). *Defining principal leadership in an era of teacher empowerment.* Paper presented at the annual meeting of the American Educational Research Association, Chicago.

Mills, G. E. (1990). *A consumer's guide to school improvement* (Trends and Issues series, No. 4). Eugene, OR: ERIC Clearinghouse on Educational Management. (ERIC Document Reproduction Service No. ED-313 800)

Osterman, K. P. (1989, March). *Supervision and shared authority: A study of principal and teacher control in six urban schools.* Paper presented at the annual meeting of the American Educational Research Association, San Francisco. (ERIC Document Reproduction Service No. ED 307-678)

Reitzug, U. C., & Cross, B. E. (1994, April). *A multi-site case study of site based management in urban schools.* Paper presented at the annual meeting of the American Educational Research Association, New Orleans, LA.

Schmuck, R. A., & Runkel, P. J. (1985). *The handbook of organizational development in schools.* Palo Alto, CA: Maryfield.

Smith, W. E. (1995, April). *A case study of principal leadership dilemmas in implementing shared decision making.* Paper presented at the annual meeting of the American Educational Research Association, San Francisco.

Smyth, J. (1992). Teachers' work and the politics of reflection. *American Educational Research Journal, 29*(2), 267-300.

9

How Am I Doing?

Lessons From Feedback

The essence of leadership is not to manage or change others; it is to manage and change oneself.

—Blanton (1991, p. 9)

Prior to beginning our study, we suspected that shared-governance leadership required a metamorphosis in principals, and we found this to be true. In related research, Bredeson (1995, pp. 12-13) found that principals who significantly changed from traditional-hierarchical leadership styles to team-centered leadership styles

- ◆ *paid greater attention* to teacher and group *needs*
- ◆ *relinquished control* to others, thereby liberating themselves from the myth of administrator omnipotence
- ◆ viewed their formal leadership role as *facilitating and advising* rather than managing and controlling
- ◆ worked to create and nurture a *culture of collegial support and trust*
- ◆ *modeled* behaviors consistent with empowerment, that is, they "walked their talk"
- ◆ helped teachers and others assume *control of and responsibility* for group maintenance processes

We also suspected that this metamorphosis was related, in part, to a principal's *openness to feedback* and ability to *learn directly from experience.* Accordingly, we designed several research questions to explore the role of feedback for the principals we studied. What we found confirmed the importance of learning from feedback.

Types of Feedback

Informal

We discovered that shared-governance principals obtain feedback on their performance in a variety of ways. One such way is through *informal,* day-to-day input from teachers:

> A few of the teachers are a little afraid to give feedback. But I may just be walking up and down the halls, and I'll mention the budget talk in the faculty meeting the other day, and I'll pick up a kind of teasing thing from a teacher, who says something like, "I don't want to do that. I wish we'd do this other kind of thing." It's kind of *informal,* but we share some information. It's not like someone comes in and says, "We want to talk with you."

> We might be at a special education meeting talking with a parent, and when the parent leaves, we're *sitting there still talking* about something that came up. I'll get feedback, but it's nothing formal.

> There are *a couple people* on the staff who are closest to me who say, for example, "Don't be as vocal because people feel like something is getting crammed down their throats even though they get to vote on it." I am amazed, but I am smart enough to realize that people are saying it even though I don't think it's true. Yesterday, I removed myself from the block-scheduling task force specifically because of that perception.

Sometimes the *grapevine* is a source of informal feedback for principals:

> About shared governance, you know, *you hear small things,* little things, about my staff members telling prospective applicants what they are able to do here and how they are able to operate in this school and with this framework.

Informal feedback is also readily *volunteered* by some teachers:

They tell me every day about my performance. In the old days, I could do anything, and they might grumble and bluster and carry on, but they wouldn't dare say anything for fear of being written up. Now I am accountable to them, and I can't just go off and do things without hearing from them. Once they asked me if I had told a teacher she had to apologize to the staff for disrupting a meeting. I hadn't, but the teacher had asked me if I thought she should apologize and I said, "Yes."

They're *not afraid to talk with me at all,* maybe because I was assistant principal here, so I'm more a part of them.

The teachers are *open* and *they'll tell me exactly* what they think.

They initiate feedback on my role and performance. Once I questioned whether they really need to know, to take time to hear, about the student support team process when the year was already half over. Many people told me we needed to have someone come, even though it wasn't my intent.

Informal feedback is also actively *invited* by shared-governance principals:

I tell people, "Look, *I need to know* how you feel about things and how I'm perceived. *I need to hear* from you. Don't just tell me what you think I want to hear."

I get a lot of one-on-one feedback by *asking people straight out*! I learned a long time ago that you learn a lot from feedback, and sometimes it's surprising. I've also done anonymous surveys and other formal things.

Formal

Additional, substantive feedback on the principal's performance and on achievement of school goals is obtained through *formal* mechanisms, such as narratives, surveys of teachers and parents, and structured evaluations from a variety of groups and individuals, including consultants to the school:

I give the *Leadership Evaluation Instrument* to the teachers every year, and I get personal feedback on a personality inventory, too.

I went to a *leadership institute* and got these *forms* to send out to the staff, my boss, and other people. I tried to be honest and get a balance of people to respond.

I get *formal feedback* on my performance. For example, the teachers are asked [to respond to this statement], "My principal is available to talk with me always, sometimes, never." Visibility is another question.

Every year I ask the staff to give me some input. "Here are some things I want to do. How would you recommend that I achieve these goals?" I don't use surveys, just a *narrative feedback*.

I periodically ask the staff to *evaluate* the administrators. I also do a *needs assessment* with parents, students, and the faculty. Also, lots of visitors come in here to examine our shared-governance school as an object for study; we've gotten some pretty good feedback there.

I get real feedback from the teachers, the students, and from the parents. *Structured feedback* comes from my evaluation that is done by the superintendent.

The *league [League of Professional Schools] does a yearly evaluation* of the schools. They suggested, for example, that we include parents on the leadership council.

We had a *seminar with a consultant* who gave us a *computerized,* formal feedback program. A random selection of faculty and staff members profiled me as a leader. It's fairly sophisticated.

I asked a *consultant* to give me pointers on my leadership and administration last year. I'm having the same person come out this year so I can compare how I'm doing year to year. He also gives us an idea of how we are doing as a school with shared governance.

Principals reported that, at times, they do *not* receive sufficient *feedback* from others. They also indicated that feedback is a valuable source of information despite the fact that it is sometimes *painful*.

I still need to get *more specific feedback*. The first time I did, it really killed my ego. It hurt my feelings. Three or four people really gave it to me. It taught me a lesson, that you can't make everybody happy when you're a leader. But the feedback and the work can be rewarding.

Structured, Relevant Feedback

Most of the feedback discussed by the shared-governance principals we interviewed dealt with their leadership. Rallis and Goldring (1994, p. 23) have proposed a set of questions useful to a school team in assessing the principal's leadership processes:

◆ Do people, both inside and outside the school, understand
    what we are trying to do (our mission)?

◆ Is teacher leadership emerging?

◆ What decision-making bodies have been established in the
    school? Do they meet? How often? Are they making decisions?
    What decisions are they making? How do people feel about
    the meetings and decisions?

◆ What opportunities for growth and development have been
    established? Do people take advantage of these oppor-
    tunities? How do people feel about their participation?

◆ What links with the community have been established? Are
    school environment relations tended to?

◆ What resources have been created or tapped? How have these
    resources been manipulated?

According to Rallis and Goldring (1994), leadership for principals of shared-governance schools consists of articulating the
school's mission, establishing and supporting team decision making,
working with external constituencies, and providing resources.
Reflecting on relevant data (e.g., surveys, questionnaires, performance instruments, open discussions), they say, helps both the
instructional team and the principal understand and improve their
work.

Feedback Content

Control

Shared-governance principals receive a great deal of positive
feedback from others, and their beliefs are, for the most part,
consistent with the precepts of shared governance, including the
importance of *letting go and facilitating the work of others.* Nonethe-
less, several principals in our study were very surprised to discover
that some teachers still felt "unfree" and had complaints about the
principal:

> I have gotten feedback on how the faculty views my role in this
> shared-governance process. I am one vote, but I am a very vocal

lobbyist. Some people, however, feel that *I still control it all*—a paranoid feeling, but it's a very real feeling that has always amazed me. I still control personnel decisions, but I am willing to give up some things like that, so the feedback, which I also get from those who study our school, strikes me as strange.

In the initial phases of the shared-governance process, I was criticized as *trying to steer decisions.* Things were said like, "She already knows what she wants, and she's just trying to manipulate us." They did the best thing: They voted in very strong people to be on the team. We all whine or cry or shout and holler or whatever, but nobody feels overrun by somebody else.

Teachers . . . perceive that *I don't delegate enough,* and it surprises me that they really don't know if I want us to be involved in shared governance.

Teachers have criticized me, so I'm fighting my own natural personality, which is to be very *direct and decision oriented.* I need to allow the structures that are in place to work, and I need to not give suggestions or try to get closure. I have worked at this steadily.

Listening

As they move toward participative decision-making approaches, school administrators are required to develop skills and techniques compatible with team leadership skills that promote *group communication, consensus building, and problem solving* (Gresso & Robertson, 1992; Schlechty, 1990). Using a training tool called the Interpersonal Process Recall (IPR), Weise (1995) demonstrated the importance of developing interpersonal communication skills as a prerequisite for building *trust.* (In this method, which uses real-life interactions, administrators-in-training assess their level of skills and learn techniques to improve self-understanding, interpersonal sensitivity, and human interaction skills.) Through feedback, the principals in our study frequently found that they came up short on the crucial communication skill of *listening:*

An improvement issue [teachers mentioned] was about *listening:* "You need to slow down and listen, even though you're busy, even though the demands are great." In a way, that was positive. So I've done a lot more of that. One lady . . . drops in and says, "You got a couple minutes?" I say, "I really am busy, but I have a couple minutes for you." That means a lot to her.

Recently I learned that *I wasn't a good listener.* It was my own perception that I was a good listener, but [teachers] felt different. This year I've worked on some strategies to listen better; I even asked some trusted people to tell me some ways I can be a better listener. They said I should do less talking, call on silent members.

I've gotten feedback about *listening* more and being available to people more. People gave me some good recommendations about everything from fireside chats to drop-ins to team visits. They said, "We trust you, we like to hear your perspective on things."

I don't know exactly how I get feedback, but I do have one teacher who repeats what I say to ensure that I am listening, or she says, *"I need you to listen to me."*

Patience

Through feedback, shared-governance principals also realized the value of *patience:*

You know what they say about life being a journey, not a destination. Well, shared governance has been frustrating for me because I've realized I'm an *impatient* person. But I have learned that shared governance is a process; it's not about getting to a point. I'm learning that every day.

Now, I get a little down occasionally because democracy is *slow and frustrating.* If I were an autocrat, I could snap my fingers and make things happen. Of course, some people would resist that, too, and the degree of satisfaction would be lower for everyone. I remind myself that this is a democratic setting, and the literature is full of examples of teachers being far more likely to make things happen when they are involved in decision making.

I'm very task oriented, and I'm not a touchy-feely person. I've been criticized in a nice way about being a workaholic, and my husband has noted that I will spend Saturday at home doing schoolwork, but I have 60 hours worth of work to do in 48 hours per week. A parent said to me, "You're not working yourself to death, are you?" That's the reputation I have in the community. But now I have really made a concerted effort to *mellow* out, to see that things may have taken a little longer, but they have happened. I counsel myself that I don't have to be pushing so hard all the time.

Governance Process Issues

Other constructive feedback focused on a range of *governance process issues:*

A teacher came in one day after school and said *she didn't like* the way a decision went. I said, "I'm sorry, but I didn't either. But *it's what the faculty decided,* and both of us will get over this." Once in a while, they'll say I don't need to bring something to them—it takes too long, and I should just decide it.

Parents have complained because we no longer have a schoolwide detention hall. *"Why don't you do something about that?"* they ask. It's hard to explain that what we do as a staff is try to find out what works and what does not work. In this case we found a better way to discipline students—parents have to come in.

They said, "We'd like to see you in a *presentation role*—for you to teach us." It was a real compliment.

Lessons Learned

Becoming a shared-governance principal requires a dramatic metamorphosis—indeed, for many, a *continuous* metamorphosis. It requires responsiveness to feedback, and even courage. It is about *self* as leader in a context of helping others become leaders; it is a process of learning *lessons.*

What Is a Lesson?

According to the principals we studied, a lesson has several dimensions, the first of which is that it involves *continual struggle.* Second, a lesson is frequently learned through *trial and error;* principals make mistakes and sometimes hurt others as well as themselves. The third dimension of a lesson is that it requires *courage* plus critical *reflection.* Fourth, and perhaps most important, is that it requires intellectual, emotional, spiritual, and behavioral *integration;* principals must "walk the talk." Excerpts from our interviews illustrate these dimensions of a lesson:

It's *not as easy as we thought it was going to be.* You have to spend some time on the lower levels of Maslow's hierarchy before you can really make a difference in the lives of children.

It's *not a continuous journey up;* it's a journey of going here and there and sometimes even backing up. It's also a frustrating and slow process, but it's personally rewarding and rewarding instructionally.

I learned that *it takes a long time* to create a vision and that shared governance *cannot be mandated*. It has to be something that is wanted and believed in by all the staff. And it *needs to be continually revisited* because we are growing and changing all the time.

It's *not something that just happens*. Everybody needs training—not just the team but the whole staff.

There's an element of risk with the board and the superintendent. We tried to change the paradigm beforehand, and to get their support. *You have to know which way the political wind is blowing.* We also got attention from other people outside the school. It was low keyed, and then we got into the limelight.

To be effective, shared-governance philosophy, including a focus on students as well as one's own perspective on leadership, must be internalized:

A lot of teachers' first feeling about shared governance is that it's going to make things better for them, not for kids. We have to help them work through that to get the *impact on the kids*.

You cannot describe shared governance to people and then make them do it. *You've got to live it,* and you've got to be patient.

You've got to internalize it, practice it, not break that trust factor. The staff is watching to see if you practice what you preach.

Backing Off and Stepping In

With few exceptions, our research suggests that shared-governance principals must successfully navigate two domains of leadership—*backing off* and *stepping in*. Stepping in, of course, is the essence of effective traditional leadership; it often involves using one's influence at the appropriate time. Given the seemingly contradictory nature of these two domains, it is not surprising that principals have difficulty maintaining a balance in the day-to-day world of the school. They learn many lessons about *backing off* and *stepping in:*

- ◆ Balancing multiple considerations
- ◆ Timing
- ◆ Control of self
- ◆ Patience

- ◆ Respect for others
- ◆ Self-understanding
- ◆ An understanding of school context
- ◆ Political skill in, for example, negotiation, persuasion, and bargaining

The following examples reflect the essence of *backing off.* (See Chapter 3 for a more complete discussion.)

A lot of it is give and take, *knowing when to sit back* and allow others to take charge and when to assert yourself. You've just got to *balance* that as best you can, because I'm not sure you ever have a script as to when to do what. Each *situation is different,* too; at some meetings I felt I had to dominate, and at other meetings I felt I should just not say anything. You just have to get a read for things.

Even though I know what I want, I've learned that *I don't have all the answers.* And everyone has something to offer, everybody's got to play a part. My overall objective is to have the best school possible; everybody has a role in that, and everybody is equally important.

I'm still learning to go back to the instructional council and say, "This crossed my desk. What do you think about it?" *I try to share* as much as I possibly can, and not just make the decision.

Once you agree that you're going to share a decision and a decision has been made, *you must accept it* whether you truly agree or not.

One thing I know is that you have to follow the shared-governance rules [procedures and agreements]. One time I was gotten out of a principals' meeting at the central office for a phone call from our teachers. I didn't intend to, but I had violated a rule. *I said, "You're right, I broke the rule,* and all I can say is, 'I'm sorry.' I can try to undo the damage." They said, "We'll tell you how to fix it." *I backed up* and did it right, even though it was not convenient. Otherwise it undercuts the process (and their trust).

When you diffuse the power, and you give it up to the teachers and the staff, any lack of maturity on your part will make you start to worry that "Maybe they don't need me." You have a tendency to want to go in with guns blazing to show that you've still got it; I've done that on an occasion or two. You get tired, and *you start to feel like you're kind of left out,* and then suddenly a minor issue comes along and *you just hit it* with both barrels. Well, *it creates more problems than it's worth.*

THE FIRE IS BACK!

At the same time, shared-governance principals learn to *step in* when necessary. This seemed easier for them than stepping back.

> You've also got to be wise enough to *know when you've got to step in* because shared governance won't work on an issue.

> Sometimes you get a group of people who come together and just won't do something or just won't compromise. You have to be wise enough to monitor everything and *step in when it is necessary*. It takes guts, but you have to do it.

> I'm looking for the best delivery of instruction, so I'm heavy into evaluation of instructional techniques and practice. That's not necessarily delegated to others; *it's not always open for feedback.*

I Have Learned . . .

As a final question in our study, we asked the principals to identify their *primary* lesson on the road to shared governance. In their words,

> *Patience.* It takes 3 to 5 years to really become a shared-governance school.

> To always treat teachers *professionally.*

> To be *honest* and to *listen.*

> That *communication* is very important.

> To *read* more so I can stay abreast of what's going on.

> That shared governance is an *ongoing process* of monitoring your own communication, of *adjusting and readjusting,* and reflecting. I've got a laptop computer, a notebook, and I've been writing things in it as I reflect. I thought about writing something about action research, "the practitioner's way."

> To never say that I have been "recognized" because I know that without teachers' hard work I would never be recognized for anything.

> That there are *people who are going to knock you down* with this thing, who will say, "I don't want to do that." They get ugly, but you've got to keep the idea in front of you and nurture it in your own life. You think [the teachers are thinking], "We don't need you here if we're making all the decisions; what do we need you for, then?" *You've got to get well beyond that.*

References

Blanton, C. (1991). A principal's vision of excellence: Achieving quality through empowerment. *Praxis, 3*(2), 1-9.

Bredeson, P. V. (1995, April). *From gazing out the ivory tower to heavy lifting in the field: Empowerment through collaborative action research.* Paper presented at the annual meeting of the American Educational Research Association, San Francisco.

Gresso, D. W., & Robertson, M. B. (1992). The principal as process consultant: Catalyst for change. *NASSP Bulletin, 76*, 44-48.

Rallis, S., & Goldring, E. B. (1994, April). *Beyond the individual assessment of principals: School-based accountability in dynamic schools.* Paper presented at the annual meeting of the American Educational Research Association, New Orleans, LA.

Schlechty, P. C. (1990). *Schools for the 21st century.* San Francisco: Jossey-Bass.

Weise, K. (1995, October). *Interpersonal process recall: An unexpected needle in the haystack called "community of learners."* Paper presented at the annual meeting of the University Council for Educational Administration, Salt Lake City, UT.

10

One Among Equals

Sharing the Governance of a School as an Advocate and Partner

In good schools superordinates do not empower teachers; instead, teachers empower their superiors. Many of the strategies that appear to empower teachers actually empower superiors because they require teacher behavior to become more visible, thereby opening the gates through which previously hidden information about school operation can flow. [This] is a necessary step to the development of a shared ethos in a school.

—Corbett and Rossman (1994, pp. 1, 5)

The proposal that teachers take an active role in the governance of schools and that administrators work with teachers *as equals* dates back to at least 1916, with John Dewey's writings.

Bolin (1989) describes oppressive leadership in terms of the attitude of conquest, divide-and-rule tactics, manipulation, paternalism, domination, and emotional baggage (including the result of making the assumption that one's strengths depend on others' weakness). In contrast, she views empowering leadership as becoming "a co-equal with all other school personnel—not equal in function, education, or responsibility, but equal in status and worth" (p. 87).

One Among Equals

Discussion of school reform and teacher empowerment naturally addresses school leadership. Kanter (1989) describes two types of leaders commonly identified with school reform:

Transformational leaders—charismatic principals who articulate visions to transform schools that may be resistant to change. These principals become *"first among equals"* in a "community of leaders" (Leithwood, 1992). As recently as 1994, Leithwood has discussed transformational leadership for school restructuring. However, his concept reflects a "power through" approach to leadership rather than a "power with" approach (see Blase & Anderson, 1995).

"Synergy czars"—principals who foster school cultures that encourage the talents and *contributions of all* members, thereby eliciting excellent, motivated performance.

Sergiovanni (1992) explains that shared leadership, taken even a step further, emphasizes organizational *culture*. Directive leadership from principals as professionals is de-emphasized, and articulating a vision, for example, becomes a *community* task rather than a leadership task. Bredeson (1989) found evidence of such leadership when he observed teachers in one district who set faculty meeting times, agendas, and topics; ran meetings; worked directly with the superintendent and the board members; and made all public reports. The teachers he investigated were part of a *team* that included the *principal as a resource person*. Bredeson discusses the significant role changes for principals that resulted from teacher involvement in school governance:

1. The need for highly developed *communication* skills
2. Expansion of the principal's *role beyond* the school
3. Re-emphasis and *clarification of expectations* for the role of principal
4. Increased *demand for time*

Freeman, Brimhall, and Neufeld (1994) also found that principal leadership changed over time in relation to changes in teacher involvement. In the early stages of shared governance, teachers noticed that principals' actions emphasized communication of trust. After a year of reform, however, teachers were more likely to recognize the importance of the principals' nonautocratic style, tolerance for divergent points of view, nonjudgmental approach, and deliberate attempts to expand teacher empowerment.

Implications of Our Study
for Principal Preparation

The study we discuss in this book examined the experiences of exemplary shared-governance principals working in a variety of school settings. A primary implication of our findings from this study and from our previous studies on shared-governance principals is that prospective and practicing principals should reflect on their *readiness* to enact a dramatically different leadership role, one in which they share responsibility and authority with teachers and others (see Blase & Blase, 1994; Blase, Blase, Anderson, & Dungan, 1995). The following points may provide guidance:

1. *Principals should consider basic assumptions.* Broadly speaking, readiness requires that the principal reflect on several fundamental *assumptions* that provide the foundation for the development of shared governance and a facilitative-democratic approach to leadership:

- The school is a learning community in which leaders become teachers and teachers become leaders.
- Schools are complex social organizations.
- The bureaucratic nature and conservative culture of traditional schools create challenges and difficulties for the development of new forms of governance.

2. Principals should *examine their fundamental beliefs about teaching.* Principals should consider whether their beliefs about teachers and teaching are consistent with those revealed in the actions of successful shared-governance principals and discussed by the teachers with whom they work. Such beliefs include the following (see Blase & Blase, 1994; Conley, 1988, pp. 7-10):

- Teachers create pedagogical *knowledge in action*; thus, the primary control of pedagogical actions should be left to teachers.
- Teaching activities are *variable and nonroutine*; thus, they require innovation and experimentation rather than meaningless standardization.

- Teachers' primary work activity is *making decisions* in highly unpredictable and interactive situations; thus, a variety of creative and sophisticated solutions is required.
- Teacher *self-esteem, confidence, ownership, autonomy, and reflection* are essential to strong instructional programs.

3. *Consider your school's context.* In addition to reflecting on the kinds of assumptions and beliefs described above, principals should reflect on *school contexts* before embarking on shared-governance initiatives. Toward this end, the following questions might be useful:

- What school, staff, community and district factors might *facilitate and hinder* the initiation and implementation of shared governance? In what ways will bureaucracy, tradition, school conditions, and discomfort with new roles constrain efforts to democratize the school?
- What are the *readiness* levels (e.g., level of trust, status of structures) of the faculty and staff to engage in collegial decision making?
- Do teachers regularly *seek and offer* help, support, and advice about teaching? Do *opportunities* for such sharing exist?
- What democratic-facilitative leadership approaches and *strategies* would be most effective in working with a particular group of teachers at a specific time?

4. Principals should *consider their own knowledge and skills related to*

- Developing *teachers' skills* to gather data, make decisions, and solve problems
- Freely engaging in *critical discourse* in which educators discuss and debate
- Recognizing *teachers* as subject-area and pedagogical *experts*
- Involving themselves as a *peer and equal* in the educational enterprise with teachers, students, parents, and others in the community

Regarding the last point, we emphasize that our findings (and those of other studies of school reform) point out that parents and other community members tend to be only minimally involved in school-level decision making. Nevertheless, the importance of fully involving such individuals is discussed frequently throughout the professional literature.

Even though all of the principals in our study became involved in shared governance *voluntarily,* they reported that they still had much to learn about implementing shared governance in general and about facilitative-democratic leadership in particular. For instance, they discovered that although many of their personal skills and values are consistent with shared governance, they still needed to make fundamental changes in self and leadership approach.

Most of the principals we studied had to learn how to step back, when to step in, and how to facilitate rather than direct. They also had to learn that even when they attempt to share power, some teachers will perceive them as manipulative or directive. They found that they were stung by teachers' criticisms and that they were not needed in as many ways as before. They learned that shared governance is difficult and time-consuming. Without exception, the principals we studied are constantly learning about themselves, others, and the process and structure of shared governance, all of which are in a constant state of flux. Indeed, shared governance requires much more of "self" (e.g., values and dispositions) than traditional school leadership. Shared governance *requires* virtuous, courageous, honest leaders.

Our last research question asked the principals in our study to share their perceptions of the *musts* of leading in facilitative-democratic ways. Their succinct responses, echoed repeatedly through our research, are found in Figures 10.1 and 10.2.

Reitzug (1994) and Bridges (1992) recommend that aspiring and practicing administrators address the *ethical* issues related to unequal power relationships with teachers, practice *problematizing* aspects of practice and policy, and develop a wide *knowledge base* to stimulate critique of practice and consideration of alternative modes of practice. As demonstrated in our study, to empower, leaders must also have an understanding of *group dynamics and conflict management* and must encourage others to refine communication, decision-making, and problem-solving skills.

Johnson's 1993 study has direct implications for the preparation of administrators (and teachers) for shared-governance leadership.

IN THEIR OWN WORDS:
"SHARED-GOVERNANCE PRINCIPALS *MUST* . . ."

- Believe in democracy
- Value democracy
- Value collegiality
- Believe that teachers can do it better: "I get real frustrated with people who go out and spend good money for a discipline package for their school when they've got good, knowledgeable teachers sitting in there working with kids every day. They know every trick in the book. With some leadership, they can do it themselves."
- Have an authentic belief in teachers: "Some young people running around here have better ideas than I've got."
- Believe that everyone can lead, not necessarily all the time but in appropriate situations
- Think through (reflect on) their vision
- Have a positive attitude
- Have the attitude that shared governance is good for people
- Listen to and respect others and believe that everybody's opinion is important
- Like people
- Learn to be less competitive
- Be willing to share power
- Make it their lifestyle: It's almost theological, believing in it
- Read more, keep up with educational innovations
- Reflect
- Practice giving it up and stepping back
- Adjust and readjust
- Begin a dialogue with teachers
- Be open and honest; say what's on their mind
- Be comfortable with who they are
- Impart their knowledge but only to a point where they can reach consensus
- Be careful not to dominate
- Be tolerant and accepting: "I can live with anything as long as it's legal, ethical, and moral."
- Learn how to develop trust
- Have a sense of right and wrong, and be consistent
- Be willing to change, and be willing to admit they're wrong

---

Figure 10.1.

- ◆ Be patient
- ◆ Be flexible
- ◆ Be mature
- ◆ Know who they are and who they are comfortable with
- ◆ Do action research
- ◆ Talk to others who are trying to do this
- ◆ Get what others are doing validated and reinforced
- ◆ Realize that it's developmental
- ◆ Be committed: "I give a lot to this school because I feel a part of it. Others do, too. If someone says something negative, it ruffles our feathers. We love this school, we share, and we're very protective of our turf. We still have the same philosophy we've had for the last 20 years."

"SHARED-GOVERNANCE PRINCIPALS *SHOULD NOT . . .*"

- ◆ Go behind and change teachers' decisions
- ◆ Take back authority once given
- ◆ Be manipulative, but they must be strategic and diplomatic
- ◆ Be arrogant: "You've got to be humble and always step aside and say, 'These are the people who have done that. It wasn't me.' "

Figure 10.1. Continued

Her work points out that principals must be able to recognize, value, and facilitate the leadership of others in instructional, professional, and organizational areas. Specifically, Johnson recommends that administrators be able to (a) arrange forums wherein others bring forth instructional and curriculum expertise and (b) assist others in reading, interpreting, and utilizing research to guide practice. Johnson also recommends that departments of curriculum, teacher education, and educational leadership be combined within colleges of education, in view of the changing roles of administrators and teachers. We agree with Rogers (1968), who wrote that it is "fruitless . . . to simply transfer power . . . without training" (p. 480).

One of the most important aspects of preparation for principals is *development of self,* which encompasses a capacity to take risks, listen to others, be authentic in relationships, and be aware of who one is as a person (Davis & Wilson, 1994). Such development is

---

**IN THEIR OWN WORDS:
"SHARED-GOVERNANCE PRINCIPALS
ADVISE OTHERS TO . . ."**

- Value others
- Respect others' beliefs
- Think of teachers as equals
- Become interpersonally astute so they can bring out the best and not put someone down; learn tact, diplomacy
- Have a very positive attitude and listen to what people say; solicit what's on their minds
- Read what others feel and think
- Learn to listen and to be honest when they disagree; learn to communicate parameters
- Watch body language, tone, and communication
- Learn how to say, "I'm sorry," and then to redo it differently
- Open up and look on a broader scale: "We're studying the future, change mechanisms, leadership, health services, community resources, and other things *with* our teachers. The Teachers as Leaders program is a model program."
- Visit shared-governance schools and talk with teachers, students, leaders, and parents; then listen to what they have to say
- Learn from resource people how the school, the community, and the region are going to change in the next 20 years
- Look for knowledge and bring it back to the faculty
- Use outside consultants
- Teach college classes to keep themselves on their toes, to keep abreast of the literature and formal preparation

---

Figure 10.2.

self-empowering and helps a leader focus on valid and productive actions. This is similar to Prawat's (1991) internally focused "conversation with self," wherein teachers develop inquiry skills, critical reflection skills, and even sociopolitical insights through internal dialogue.

We asked the principals in our study to recommend essential elements of an effective shared-governance principal preparation program. This is what they said *in general:*

An aspiring shared-governance principals program needs to provide *field experiences* with shared-governance schools. They need to go and work at those schools for a quarter. School boards need to make the commitment to give these people leave to do that.

I don't know if there is any formal way of *acquiring those skills* because I'm not sure what I'm able to do here could be done by another principal—or that I could be effective in that other position. You can't do it exactly the same way; you just acquire your skills as you go along.

They must be taught that it's *situational,* with a need for flexibility meshed in there.

Learn about the *pitfalls,* the kinds of *roadblocks* and *problems* they will face. They need to know what to expect, since they have all the accountability.

On structure:

They need to go through an *assessment* of their skills, like the NASSP Assessment Program.

Get the current successful shared-governance principals into *graduate preparation programs* to share their knowledge in seminars.

Have a *symposium of leaders.* Have a conversation about things they faced and how they handled issues.

Have a *leadership academy.*

Have experienced shared-governance principals *train* others.

Have *role playing* in training.

Make it *real.* It affects your ego, and you have to be able to take criticism.

Intern under at least two people with different leadership styles.

On curriculum:

Understand the shared-governance *philosophy.*

Create a course, some real *pedagogy* of how you *do* shared governance, how shared governance works.

Read Lincoln on *leadership,* Attila the Hun on leadership, Demming's principles, others on *democracy.*

Study leadership *styles.*

Study the difference between *traditional* and *shared* governance leadership.

Prepare and train in *action research* and statistics.

Learn creative ways to use *resources*.

Learn *human relations* knowledge or be constantly frustrated.

Learn *group skills*: communication, facilitation skills, building trust, organizing meetings, partnering, conflict management, decision making, and problem-solving skills and training, listening skills. ("I need the ability to communicate with my staff, whether verbally or nonverbally. If you have all the book knowledge in the world, but you cannot communicate or your philosophies are different, it won't work.")

Learn about *instruction and innovative programs*.

Learn how to *collaborate*.

Learn to *network*, to *share problems and successes*.

Learn *team building and facilitation* skills—how to draw people out, how to share—and open up yourself.

Learn about *change*.

Develop expertise in *reading situations*.

Learn how to determine the *community's expectations* and what kind of *community support* mechanisms are in place.

Preparing Teacher Leaders

Teachers in shared-governance settings must become leaders, too. However, as Lonnquist and King (1993) note, "The leaders of innovative, forward-thinking schools are called upon to be, in essence, organizational consultants and futurists. Finding teachers with these rare skills can be challenging given the predominant teacher training and teacher responsibility paths at this time" (p. 25). This, of course, means that principals face the added challenge of developing teacher talent.

In recent research, teacher participation in shared governance has been related to several factors: (a) the degree to which principals believe such participation is important to student achievement, (b) their confidence that teachers have the necessary knowledge and skills to make key decisions, (c) and their belief that teachers themselves have the authority to make key decisions (Ganopole, 1991). These findings suggest that principals should have access to funds and support for professional programs to help teachers learn about attitudes, values, and techniques consistent with shared approaches to school governance.

For example, leadership team training would be a useful tool for principals in developing teacher reflection. Training might include such topics as group development and development of action research skills. School leadership teams are more likely to address issues of significance if (a) minor faculty concerns are resolved first; (b) teams are able to do their own work through formal structures for goal setting, determining agendas, and reaching decisions; (c) adequate numbers of people have a stake in the outcome and are involved in prioritizing concerns; and (d) the database for generating concerns, alternatives, and solutions is both comprehensive and objective (Kirby, 1991, pp. 14-15).

Prawat (1991) notes that the *key* to empowerment is *nurturing alternative modes of discourse.* This includes creating a supportive environment in which people can discover and express their own voices. It also means making people aware of how schools perpetuate unequal power arrangements between educators, on the one hand, and community members, on the other. McDonald's 1986 study of the history of a teacher-empowerment project illustrates the various agendas that emerged in a team over the course of a year, as members grew in their ability to reflect on their work:

Phase 1: Teachers groped to find a voice, a language for talking with each other.

Phase 2: Teachers' talk was aimed at finding a professional voice. They saw their earlier silence as a protective response to their lack of autonomy and their subordination; it reflected more than isolation and low status.

Phase 3: The focus shifted to the need to frame one's work to gain order and perspective on the complex business of teaching. Reflective anecdotes were used to test of theories to make sense out of specific situations and to change the ways the teachers understood and experienced practice.

Zeichner and Tabachnick (1991) have described four types of reflective practice, each with a different focus. It would be helpful for teachers to look at the priorities, philosophies, and historical traditions of each of the following types of reflective practice:

1. *Academic* reflective practice stresses understanding and translation of subject matter for student learning.
2. *Social efficiency-oriented* reflective practice emphasizes the thoughtful use of teaching strategies suggested by research.
3. *Developmentalist* reflective practice emphasizes teaching that is sensitive to students' interests, thinking, and developmental growth.
4. *Social reconstructionist* reflective practice stresses reflection about how the social and political context of schools and classroom evaluation have affected equity, social justice, and humane conditions in schools and society.

Checking Ourselves

Finally, we note that in their study of school reform in Chicago, Rollow and Bryk (in press) created clusters of indicators for the salient features of local school governance. Principal leadership in democratic reforms is characterized, for example, by the following:

1. Priority use of time on personal development, teacher/staff development, and working with parent and community groups.
2. A leadership style that realizes that conflict is necessary for change, a reliance on committees to resolve conflict, support of structured teacher input, and support for teachers in assuming administrative tasks.
3. A broad role for faculty in budget planning and hiring of professional staff.

Indicators of collective faculty activity included teacher voice, teacher influence, joint work, and shared decision making.

We suggest that these findings, in a broad way, and our findings reported in this book, in a more specific way, can guide the work of

principals practicing facilitative/democratic leadership. Indeed, we
believe that this nation's core belief in democracy *requires* shared
governance of schools, collective efforts to improve schools, and
exemplary leadership. We hope that the courageous principals who
poignantly revealed to us their successes and their disappointments
along the road to democratic schooling have sparked in our readers
that all-important fire, that determination to renew our schools.

References

Blase, J., & Anderson, G. (1995). *The micropolitics of educational leadership.* New York: Teachers College Press.

Blase, J., & Blase, J. R. (1994). *Empowering teachers: What successful
principals do.* Thousand Oaks, CA: Corwin.

Blase, J., Blase, J., Anderson, G., & Dungan, S. (1995). *Democratic principals in action: Eight pioneers.* Thousand Oaks, CA: Corwin.

Bolin, F. S. (1989). Empowering leadership. *Teachers College Record, 91*(1),
81-96.

Bredeson, P. V. (1989). Redefining leadership and the roles of school:
Responses to changes in the professional work-life of teachers. *High
School Journal, 23*(1), 9-20.

Bridges, E. M. (1992). *Problem based learning for administrators.* Eugene:
University of Oregon. (ERIC Document Reproduction Service No. ED
347 617)

Conley, S. C. (1988, April). *From school site management to "participatory
school site management."* Paper presented at the annual meeting of the
American Educational Research Association, New Orleans, LA.

Corbett, H. D., & Rossman, G. B. (1994, April). *How teachers empower
superordinates: Running good schools.* Paper presented at the annual
meeting of the American Educational Research Association, New Orleans, LA.

Davis, J. H., & Wilson, S. M. (1994, April). *The relationship of principal
empowering behaviors to teacher motivation, job satisfaction, and job
stress.* Paper presented at the annual meeting of the American Educational Research Association, New Orleans, LA.

Freeman, D. J., Brimhall, P. A., & Neufeld, J. (1994, April). *Who's in charge
now? A principal's endeavors to empower teachers.* Paper presented at
the annual meeting of the American Educational Research Association,
New Orleans, LA.

Ganopole, S. J. (1991, April). *A comparison of public and private school
principals' perceptions of and attitude toward teacher participation in
the management of schools.* Paper presented at the annual meeting of
the American Educational Research Association, Chicago.

Johnson, M. (1993, April). *Defining and negotiating leadership roles: Leadership from Hollibrook Elementary School.* Paper presented at the annual meeting of the American Educational Research Association, Atlanta, GA.

Kanter, R. M. (1989). *When giants learn to dance: Mastering the challenges of strategy, management, and careers in the 1990s.* New York: Simon & Schuster.

Kirby, P. C. (1991, April). *Shared decision making: Moving from concerns about restrooms to concerns about classrooms.* Paper presented at the annual meeting of the American Educational Research Association, Chicago.

Leithwood, K. A. (1992). The move toward transformational leadership. *Educational Leadership, 49*(5), 8-12.

Lonnquist, M. P., & King, J. A. (1993, April). *Changing the tire on a moving bus: Barriers to the development of professional community in a new teacher-led school.* Paper presented at the annual meeting of the American Educational Research Association, Atlanta.

McDonald, J. P. (1986). Raising the teacher's voice and the ironic role of theory. *Harvard Educational Review, 56*(4), 355-378.

Prawat, R. S. (1991). Conversations with self and settings: A framework for thinking about teacher empowerment. *American Educational Research Journal, 28*(4), 737-757.

Reitzug, U. C. (1994). A case study of empowering principal behavior. *American Educational Research Journal, 31*(2), 283-307.

Rogers, D. (1968). *110 Livingston Street.* New York: Random House.

Rollow, S. G., & Bryk, A. S. (in press). Politics as a lever for organizational change. In A. S. Bryk, J. Q. Easton, D. Kerbow, S. G. Rollow, & P. Sebring (Eds.), *Democratic participation and organizational change: The Chicago school experience.* Boulder, CO: Westview.

Sergiovanni, T. J. (1992). Why we should seek substitutes for leadership. *Educational Leadership, 49*(5), 41-45.

Zeichner, K., & Tabachnick, B. (1991). Reflections on reflective teaching. In B. Tabachnick & K. Zeichner (Eds.), *Issues and practice in inquiry-oriented teacher education* (pp. 2-3). London: Falmer.

Resource A:
Research Method
and Procedures

This book portrays exemplary principals' perspectives on shared governance leadership in a variety of schools that are members of the League of Professional Schools. A description of the research questions used in our study and the methods and procedures used to gather data from principals are provided here.

The Study

Participant Selection Process

From recommendations by League of Professional Schools participants and facilitators and University of Georgia faculty working with the league, a pool of 18 exemplary principals was selected. Recommendations were based on reports of a principal's success in using facilitative-democratic leadership in implementing shared governance in public school settings in Georgia.

Demographic data were compiled for each of the 18 exemplary candidates. Nine principals were selected for participation in our study on the basis of achieving the broadest possible representation of race and gender and on school-setting diversity across the elementary, middle school, and high school levels. The study sample consisted of male ($n = 4$) and female ($n = 5$), white ($n = 6$) and African American ($n = 3$) principals from rural ($n = 2$), suburban ($n = 6$), and urban ($n = 1$) school settings. Three elementary, four middle, and two high schools were represented by the nine principals. The average age of participating principals was 46; the average number of years in the principalship was 12; the average number of years in the principalship in the school studied was 9. Degrees earned were EdS ($n = 3$), EdD ($n = 4$) and PhD ($n = 2$). Each participant was contacted by a researcher, and the scope and purpose of the study were explained. All of these principals were considered exemplary shared-governance leaders (per league and peer assessments), and all agreed to voluntary, uncompensated participation in our study.

Data Collection

Data were collected and analyzed in accordance with symbolic interaction theory. Although this theoretical approach recognizes that structural factors influence action, it emphasizes the meanings that people assign to action. In essence, people's reflexivity is given more importance than structural factors. Through social action, the individual is influenced but maintains distance from others and is capable of initiating individual action (Blumer, 1969; Mead, 1934). Symbolic interactionism, in contrast to some approaches to qualitative research, stresses individual perception and interpretation (Blumer, 1969).

The study discussed in this book examined the broad question, "What are the principal's perspectives on facilitative-democratic leadership and shared governance in schools?" An initial protocol of 12 open-ended interview questions focusing on the nature of leadership and shared governance was developed by the researchers. These questions explored, from the principals' perspectives, the following topics:

1. Meanings attributed to shared governance
2. Precipitants to involvement in shared governance
3. Formal governance structures and processes
4. Parental and student involvement in shared governance
5. The process of developing shared vision
6. The process of principal role change in shared governance
7. Feedback on principal role and performance
8. Issues related to being a leader and partner in shared decision making
9. Maintenance of a focus on curriculum and instruction
10. Personal and professional effects of being a shared governance principal
11. Lessons learned about facilitative-democratic leadership and shared governance
12. Skills, knowledge, attitudes, and values required to enact leadership for shared governance

Data were collected over 7 months during the 1994-1995 academic year. A researcher spent several hours in site-based conferences and telephone conferences with each participating principal.

Interview dates were scheduled, at the principals' convenience, with all nine principals at their schools. During the interviews, principals were asked to provide basic background information about themselves and their schools. The interviews followed the open-ended protocol questions identified above but also allowed for follow-up and clarification. The interviews were audiotaped by the researcher. Following each interview, audiotapes were reviewed for quality and transcribed. Researchers then reviewed transcriptions for accuracy.

Data Analysis

Interview data were analyzed according to guidelines for grounded theory inquiry and constant comparative analysis (Glaser, 1978; Glaser & Strauss, 1967). This approach to analysis requires a comparison of each new unit of data with those coded previously for emergent categories and subcategories. Specifically, data related to each of the research questions were clustered for all principals studied. The latter procedure produced categories and themes characteristic of the entire database. Data from the interviews are used throughout this book to illustrate selected ideas (quotes have been edited slightly for succinctness and clarity). To preserve the principals' anonymity, names have been omitted.

References

Blumer, H. (1969). *Symbolic interactionism: Perspective and method.* Englewood Cliffs, NJ: Prentice Hall.

Glaser, B. G. (1978). *Theoretical sensitivity: Advances in the methodology of grounded theory.* Mill Valley, CA: Sociology Press.

Glaser, B. G., & Strauss, A. L. (1967). *The discovery of grounded theory: Strategies for qualitative research.* Chicago: Aldine.

Mead, G. H. (1934). *Mind, self, and society.* Chicago: University of Chicago Press.

Subject Index